STUDIES IN THE BOOK
BY REVERE FRANKLIN WEIDNER

Just
SINNER

www.JustandSinner.com

STUDIES IN THE BOOK
BY REVERE FRANKLIN WEIDNER

Just & Sinner
515 E. Lincoln Ave.
Watseka, IL

www.JustandSinner.com

ISBN 10: 0692299181
ISBN 13: 9780692299180

Original Publishing Info:

REVERE FRANKLIN WEIDNER.
Professor and Doctor of Theology.
Prepared for Use of the Students of the Bible Institute, Chicago.
Dwight L. Moody, President.
CHICAGO: 148 and 150 Madison Street.

NEW YORK:
12 Bible House, Astor Place.

Entered according to Act of Congress, in the year 1890, by
FLEMING H. REVELL,
In the Office of the Librarian of Congress, at Washington, D.C.

Dedication:
TO   DWIGHT L. MOODY, WHOSE LABORS FOR THE
SALVATION OF THE NEGLECTED POOR ARE EQUALLED BY
THE SIMPLICITY AND POWER IN WHICH HE PRESENTS THE
TRUTHS OF THE GOSPEL, THESE STUDIES IN THE BOOK
ARE MOST RESPECTFULLY DEDICATED BY THE AUTHOR.

CONTENTS OF STUDIES.

INTRODUCTION.

George Henry Gerberding called Weidner's *Studies in the Book* his most original contribution to theology. These volumes, covering the entirety of the New Testament and parts of the Old, are based on lectures given by Weidner to students at the Moody Bible Institute in Chicago, IL. In them, he gives outlines of Scriptural books, emphasizing their primary teachings and theological themes. He gives details about the authorship and dating of each book.

This particular volume covers the four Gospels and the Catholic Epistles. Weidner also includes doctrinal chapters on each aspect of the order of salvation, as well as on Scripture and the role of the Holy Spirit. He defends the inerrancy of Holy Scripture, as well as giving a thorough defense of traditional authorship and dating for several of the doubted New Testament books.

I tried to generally keep Weidner's outline form in these chapters, but have occasionally made changes to make the text more readable. The spelling of various words have been changed to conform to contemporary usage. I have not changed Weidner's extensive harmony of the Gospels due to the difficulty of remaking the chart from the original text. Thus this chapter has been photocopied from the original edition. This book includes several reference tools for Bible study, many of which are out of print. Most of them can, however, be found on Google Books for free viewing, since they are in the public domain.

This work will be beneficial to any student of the Bible, in giving both a helpful outline of Scriptural books, as well as beneficial guidelines for the study of God's Word.

Jordan Cooper
Watseka, IL
2014

PREFACE.

These "Outline Studies" have been prepared primarily for the use of the students of "The Bible Institute" of the Chicago Evangelization Society, of which Mr. D. L. Moody is President. They cover about half the books of the New Testament, including the Four Gospels, the Acts of the Apostles, the seven General Epistles, and the Book of Revelation. An attempt has been made to guide the student to an inductive study of the Bible, and to be helpful in suggesting to him methods.

The writer has had a double purpose in view in preparing these notes; first, to be of help to the private student in his personal edification, and secondly, to furnish a textbook which in the hands of a leader may tend to promote the more exact study of God's Word among the Young Men's Christian Associations, and Societies of Christian Endeavor. For this purpose the aim has been so to present the truths and duties of God's Word as to give the earnest believer power and wisdom to do aggressive work for Christ, and lead men to salvation. It is not expected that any of these Studies are to be finished in an hour. On some, even a dozen hours may be spent profitably. In the last Study the student will find some hints as to the manner of review. Each Study, as a rule, is divided into two parts. On account of the great importance of the Biblical teaching concerning the Work of the Holy Spirit in the salvation of souls, this doctrine has been fully developed. Believing that the Bible is the Word of God, the infallible guide for our daily life, and the absolute rule of our faith, and holding that there is a unity of Biblical truth, great stress has been laid upon the exact and positive meaning of each passage, and upon the importance of the comparative study of Scripture.

K. P. W.
Augustana Theological Seminary,
Rock Island, Ill.
Epiphany, 1890.

STUDY I.
PART I.

Facts About the Book.

1. Order of books with number of chapters. (Drill.)
I.— Historical Books: Matt. (28); Mark (16); Luke (24); John (21); Acts (28).
II.— Epistles of Paul: Rom. (16); I. Cor. (16); II. Cor. (13); Gal. (6); Eph. (6); Phil. (4); Col. (4); I. Thess. (5); II. Thess. (3); I. Tim. (6); II. Tim. (4); Titus (3); Philemon (1); Heb. (13).
III.-General Epistles: James (5); I. Pet. (5); II. Pet. (3); I. John (5); II. John (1); III. John (1); Jude (1).
IV.— Prophecy: Revelation (22).

2. The Epistles of Paul in chronological order. (Drill.)
(1) 52 A.D., I. and II. Thess.; (2) 57 A.D., Gal., I. and II. Cor., Romans; (3) 62 A.D., Col., Eph., Philemon, Phil., Hebrews possibly 63 A.D.; (4) 67 A.D.. I. Tim., Titus, II. Tim.

3. Authors of the New Testament Books.
Eight different persons wrote the twenty-seven books:
Matthew, Mark. Luke (Gosp. and Acts), John (Gosp., Three Epistles and Rev.), Paul, James, Peter, Jude.

4. The books of the New Testament are genuine, i.e., they were written by the persons whose names they bear.

I.— External Evidence.
First: By our printed Bibles since the fifteenth century.
Second: By Greek manuscripts, some dating from the fourth century.
Third: By the writings of the Fathers. Eusebius, died 340 A.D., Bishop of Caesarea in Palestine; Origen, died 254 A.D., who lived in Egypt and Palestine; Tertullian, died 220 A.D., who lived at Carthage in North Africa; Clemens, of Alexandria, in Egypt, died 220 A. D.;

Irenaeus, of Smyrna in Asia Minor, afterward Bishop of Lyons in France, died 202 A.D.; Polycarp, the teacher of Irenaeus, who himself was a pupil of St. John. All these bear witness to the fact that the books of the New Testament were written by the authors whose names they bear.

II. — Internal Evidence.
This results from a special study of each book, and refers to the language, style and peculiar historical allusions of each writer.

5. Our copies of the New Testament are correct and accurate. We have a correct copy of the original Greek text.

First. We have about two thousand manuscripts, containing larger or smaller portions of the Greek Testament, dating from the fourth to the sixteenth century.

Second: The many variations, averaging about ninety to a manuscript, strange as it may seem, enable us to restore, with certainty, the very words of the Apostles.

Third. We have today a text of the Greek Testament as near the primitive text of the Apostles as the organized efforts of the scholarship and criticism of the present age, assisted by Divine help, can determine.

Fourth. There are three such critical texts, of a very high order, differing only in minor points,— those of Tischendorf, of Tregelles, and of Westcott and Hort.

III. — Our translations fairly and accurately reproduce this Greek text.
First: Translations were made because those to whom its truths were preached did not understand Greek.
Second: Among the Ancient Versions we may mention:
(1) The Syriac or Peshito, second century; (2) the Old Latin, second century; (3) the Egyptian, third century; (4) the Ethiopic, fourth century; (5) the Gothic, fourth century; (6) the Latin Vulgate of Jerome, fourth century; (7) the Armenian, fifth century; (8) the Arabic, eighth century; (9) the Slavonic, ninth century.

Third: Among the principal Modern Versions, not including the English, we may mention:
(1) the Italian, 1471: (2) Luther's German, 1522; (3) the Dutch, 1526; (4) the Swedish, 1526; (5) the French, 1530; (6) the Icelandic, 1540; (7) the Spanish, 1543; (8) the Danish, 1550; (9) the Portuguese, 1712.

Fourth: The Revised English Version of the New Testament.
(1) The English translation of the Bible has a growth, and is the result of the labors and scholarship of four centuries.
(2) Among the English translations we may mention:

> 1. Wiclif's New Testament, about 1380 — before printing was invented.
> 2. Tyndale's New Testament, 1526 — the first printed edition of any part of the Scriptures in English.
> 3. Miles Coverdale's Bible, 1535— the first English Bible printed by authority.
> 4. Matthew's Bible, 1537 — a reproduction of Tyndale's New Testament — Matthew being the name assumed by John Rogers, the martyr.
> 5. Taverner's Bible, 1539— a correction of Matthew's Bible.
> 6. The Great Bible, 1539— revised by Cranmer and Coverdale. The edition of 1540 contains a preface by Cranmer and is known as Cranmer's Bible.
> 7. The Geneva Bible, 1560 (New Testament, 1557) published by English exiles in Geneva, especially revised by Coverdale and John Knox, with notes favoring the peculiar doctrines of Calvin.
> 8. The Bishop's Bible, 1568 — so-called because eight Bishops assisted in this revision.
> 9. The Rhemish New Testament, 1582 — published by Romanists at Rheims, France, containing many foreign words and difficult phrases, making it almost unintelligible to the common people — still the Authorised Version of the Roman Catholic Church.
> 10. King James's Bible, 1611 — known as the Authorized English Version.
> 11. The Revised Version of 1881.

(3) The differences between the Authorized and Revised Versions arise from two causes:

1. Alterations made on account of a change of the reading of the Greek text, (a) The Authorized Version was made from printed Greek Testaments not representing the purest text now attainable, (b) The Revised Version is a faithful translation of the purest text at present attain able.

2. Alterations made on account of a change of the translation of the Greek text, (a) There has been a progress in Greek scholarship, (b) Some English words have become obsolete or changed in meaning (c) A more exact translation was demanded, (d) In the Revised Text we have the New Testament in a form more nearly identical with the primitive text of the Apostles than ever before, (e) Possibly it may seem too literal to those very familiar to the Authorized Version. (f) The two versions ought to be used side by side, (g) The importance and value of the Revised Version.

6. The importance of the study of the Greek New Testament to Biblical students.

7. But let us not forget that a thoughtful and pious English reader is able to understand the New Testament better than many who read it in Greek.

PART II.
The Doctrine of the Holy Spirit.

I. God has revealed himself as one in divine essence, but as subsisting in three persons — a Unity in Trinity. This is a great mystery.

First: The unity of God is distinctly taught in Scripture. Deut. I: 33; 6: 4; 2 Sam. 7: 22; Ps. 88: 10; Isa. 43: 10. 11; Mark 12: 29; John 17: 3; 1 Cor. 8: 4; Eph. 4: 6.

Second: This unity is one of divine essence.

Third: The doctrine of the Trinity is also clearly taught— that God, one in essence, subsists in three persons, truly and really distinct from each other.

(a) We have a manifestation to human senses of the separate existence of the three persons in the wonderful theophany at the baptism of Christ (Matt. 3: 13-17; Mark 1:9-11; Luke 3: 21, 22). (1) The voice of the Father is heard from heaven, bearing witness to his Son. (2) The Son is being baptized in the river Jordan. (3) The Holy Ghost is seen, in the form of a dove, descending upon Jesus.

(b) The doctrine of the Holy Trinity is also distinctly taught in the solemn formula of baptism given by Christ (Matt. 28: 19). We are to be baptized into the name (not names) of the one God, in three divine persons, the Father, the Son, and the Holy Ghost.

(c) The three Persons of the Holy Trinity are often mentioned together. John 14: 16; 15: 26; II. Cor. 13: 14; Rom. S: 9, 11; Eph. 2:18; 2:21, 22; 3:14-16; 4:4-6; 4:30-32, 5:18, 20; Heb. 9: 14; I. Pet. 1:2; Jude 20, 21; etc.

Fourth: The inner distinction and the relation of the Holy Ghost to the Father and the Son may be expressed by the phrase "eternal procession."

(a) The Holy Ghost proceeds from the Father. (1) It is so stated in express words, John 15:26. (2) Christ says the Father will send him in his name, John 14:26; compare Gal. 4: 6. (3) He is called the Spirit of the Father, Matt. 10: 20; compare I. Cor. 2: 10, 11; Eph. 4: 30. (b) The Holy Ghost proceeds from the Son. (1) Because he is sent and given by the Son, John 15: 26; 20: 22. (2) Because he is called the Spirit of the Son, Gal. 4: 6. (3) Because he is called the Spirit of Christ, Rom. 8:9; Phil. 1:19; I. Pet. 1:11.

Fifth: In all outward works or operations, as Creation, Redemption, Sanctification, the three persons work together, and although the outward works may be predicated of one person, the others are still not absolutely excluded.

Sixth: In outward works, however, an order and distinction
of persons may be drawn:

(a) The origin of grace is in God the Father, the Creator, Preserver, and Governor of all things, Eph. 1: 4, 6; Gen. 1:1; John 1:3.

(b) The acquisition of grace is by God the Son, the Redeemer, John 3: 10, 17.

(c) The application of grace is made by God the Holy Ghost, the Sanctifier, Rom. 15: 16.

STUDY II.
PART I.
On the Study of the New Testament.

First: The interest shown in Bible study a hopeful sign.

Second: Everything depends on the spirit in which the Bible is studied, and the object in view.

Third: We take for granted the divine authority of the Bible and the truth of Christianity.

Fourth: We are going to study the New Testament (a) as a guide for our daily life, and (b) as a rule of our faith.

Fifth: The study of the Bible, in contradistinction to the books of men, brings about a union of believers and a unity of the faith.

Sixth: There can be no unity of the faith unless there be agreement as to the fundamental principles of interpretation.

Seventh: We ought at least to agree on these principles:
   (1) God wants us to understand his word.
   (2) Every passage has but one true meaning.
   (3) The meaning of God's word is capable of being investigated.

Eighth: The student of the New Testament should be endowed with certain faculties.
   (1) Intellectual Faculties: He should have a clear and vigorous understanding, sound judgment, and a broad culture.
   (2) Moral Faculties: The irreligious interpreter is morally unfit for the task of explaining the Bible. The teacher of religion must be conscientious, circumspect and laborious.

Ninth: The student must cultivate the proper dispositions.

(1) Love of Truth: He must not come to the Bible with preconceived ideas, but ask simply, What is written? He must not only be impartial in mind, but also in heart, and seek as far as God gives him grace to become morally perfect.

(2) Search for clear ideas. The means to attain clearness are study and meditation.

Tenth: There are certain duties which he must diligently perform.

(1) His studies must embrace the entire Bible, and not only certain portions.

(2) Meditation and constant study of the scriptures are absolutely necessary to render clear, vivid and fruitful its rich treasures.

(3) Our studies ought to be continued with distrust of one's self and with a feeling of one's own weakness.

(4) The means of Bible study are: Prayer, meditation or study, and Christian experience.

Eleventh: There is a difference between reading and studying the Bible.

(1) We may read for devotion, for knowledge, or for instruction in righteousness, II. Tim. 3: 16, 17.

(2) We may read by chapters consecutively or chronologically, or by topics.

Twelfth: Two principal methods of studying the Bible:
(1) By topics. (2) By books. (3) Both methods are good. Your object in view must decide the method.

Thirteenth: Even if you wish to study the New Testament according to subjects, the best way is by books.

Fourteenth. Different kinds of books ought to be studied in different ways.

Fifteenth: General hints for the study of the Gospels:

(1) The best of method of studying the Gospel history is by means of a harmony.

(2) The Gospel of Mark deserves to be studied first in order of time.

(a) Because it supplies the best basis for constructing a harmony, being written in chronological order.

(b) It is the best introduction to the regular and systematic study of the New Testament.

(3) Study carefully the chronology and geography of each event.

(4) Compare parallel accounts by the different evangelists.

(5) Read in connection with the study of the Gospel history a good life of Christ. (Stalker, Andrews, Ellicott, Farrar, Geikie, Edersheim).

(6) Study special subjects very carefully.

(a) The Sermon on the Mountain; (b) The Parables of Christ; (c) The Miracles of Christ; (d) The Discourses of Jesus in John.

(7) Classify the doctrinal teachings of Christ.

(1) About God. (2) About Man (3) About his own Person and Work. (4) About the Way of Salvation. (5) About the Church and the Sacraments. (6) About the Last Things.

(8) Examine carefully all questions pertaining to what is known as "Introduction." For whom written? When? Where? Why?

Sixteenth: General hints for the study of the Pauline Epistles.

(1) Study carefully those parts of the Acts of the Apostles bearing on the life and labors of Paul.

(2) Read in connection some concise life of Paul. (Stalker.)

(3) Fix clearly in your mind the more prominent events of Paul's life.

(a) 37 A.D. Conversion, (b) 45 A.D. First missionary journey, (c) 50 A.D. Second missionary journey, (d) 54 A.D. Third missionary journey, (e) 62 A.D. First captivity at Rome. (f) 68 A.D. Second captivity and martyrdom.

(4) Arrange and study his letters in chronological order. (See Study I)

(5) Read in connection with your studies a fuller life of Paul. (Conybeare and Howson, or Farrar).

(6) Become perfectly familiar with the geography of Paul's labors.

Seventeenth: Special hints for the study of the Pauline Epistles.

(1) Read the Epistle carefully, at one sitting, for general contents.

(2) Read carefully a second time, noting all references bearing on questions of "Introduction." (By whom written? For whom? When? Where? Why?)

(3) Then read some Introduction to the Epistle, as found in a good Commentary, and compare results and correct.

(4) Read carefully a third time, and divide into main parts:

(1) Personal: (2) Doctrinal: (3) Practical.

(5) Read carefully a fourth time, and divide into sections. The sections as given in the Revised Version will be of great help.

(6) Study carefully each section, and write out the thought, as clearly and concisely as possible.

(7) Study the Epistle carefully, and classify the practical duties enforced.

(a) Duties to God.

(b) Duties to our fellow-man. (1) In the State. (2) In the Church. (3) In the Family,

(c) Duties to self.

(8) Study the Epistle carefully, and classify the doctrinal truths taught.

(a) The doctrine of God. Attributes, Trinity, Predestination, Creation, Providence, Good and Evil Angels, Satan.

(b) The doctrine of Man. Creation of Man, his Original Condition, his Fall, Original Sin, Essential Character of Sin, Actual Sins, Free Will.

(c) The doctrine of the Person of Christ. His Human Nature, his Divine Nature, the State of Humiliation, the State of Exaltation.

(d) The doctrine of the Work of Christ. His Mediatorial Work, his Prophetic Office, his Priestly Office, his Kingly Office, the Atonement, Resurrection of Christ, Ascension into Heaven, sitting at the Right Hand of God, his Intercession, the Kingdom of Christ.

(e) The doctrine of the Work of the Holy Spirit. Calling, Illumination, Regeneration, Conversion,

Repentance, Faith, Justification, Mystical Union, Adoption, Sanctification, Holiness, Good Works.

(f) The doctrine of the Church. Nature and Attributes of the Church, Inspiration of the Scriptures, the Means of Grace, the Word of God, Baptism, the Lord's Supper, the Ministry.

(g) The doctrine of the Last Things, Death, State of the Soul after death, Fullness of the Gentiles, Conversion of Israel, Antichrist, Second Coming of Christ, the General Resurrection, the Final Judgment, the End of the World, the Final Consummation, Eternal Death, Eternal Life.

PART II.
The Personality and Deity of the Holy Ghost.

First: The Holy Ghost is not an attribute of God, nor a mere energy of influence, but the third person of the Holy Trinity.

Second: By person we mean an intelligent agent, one who possesses personal properties.

Third: The personality of the Holy Ghost is proved by Scripture:
> (1) Personal pronouns are applied to Him. John 14:16, 17, 26; 15:26; 16:7, 13, 14, etc.
> (2) Personal qualities are ascribed to Him. He knows and searches all things. I, Cor. 2: 10, 11; He works according to His own will, I. Cor, 12:11; He can be grieved, Eph. 4: 30; He can be resisted, Acts 7:51; He can be blasphemed against, Matt. 12:31, 32; He can be lied against, Acts 5:3, 4; etc.
> (3) Personal acts are ascribed to Him. He teaches all things John 14: 26; He guides into all the truth, John 16: 13; He helpeth our infirmity, Rom. 8:26; He convicts the world, John 16:8; He sanctifies and bestows spiritual gifts, Rom. 15:16; I. Cor. 12:11; He seals, Eph. 1:13; 4:30; He comforts. Acts 9:31, etc.

Fourth: That the Holy Spirit, the third person of the Trinity, is truly divine, true God, of the same essence with the Father and the Son, is proved from the fact that to Him are ascribed:
> (1) Divine names. He is called God. Acts 5:3, 4; II. Pet. 1: 21, compared with II Tim. 3: 16; I. Cor. 3: 16; Lord, II. Cor. 3: 17; I. Cor 12. 4, 5; Jehovah, Isa. 6: 5 10; compared with Acts 28: 25, Ex. 17. 7, compared with Heb. 3: 7-9.
> (2) Divine attributes. Eternity, Heb. 9: 14; Omnipotence, I. Cor. 12. 11; Rom. 8: 11, 15: 19, Omniscience, I. Cor. 2: 10-12; Omnipresence, Ps. 139: 7; I. Cor. 12- 13; Rom. 8:26, 27.

(3) Divine works. Creation, Gen. 1:2; Job 26: 13; Ps. 33: 6; Preservation, Job 33: 4; Ps. 104: 30; Miracles, Matt. 12: 28; I. Cor. 12. 9-11, Rom. 15: 19; Resurrection, of the dead, I. Pet. 3: 18; Rom. 8:11; Prophecy, II. Pet. 1:21; II. Sam 23: 2; Works of grace, as regeneration, John 3: 5;. Titus 3: 5; Sanctification, Rom. 15: 16; I. Pet. 1:2; etc.

(4) Divine Worship, Rom. 9: 1; II. Cor. 13: 14; Matt. 28: 19.

STUDY III.
PART I.
On the Interpretation of the New Testament.

First: The interpreter must be endowed with the proper intellectual and moral faculties, and cultivate especially the proper dispositions necessary for the exposition of Scripture. (See Study II).

Second: Certain facts or principles are taken for granted. (1) The Inspiration of the Bible. (2) Each passage has but one positive meaning. (3) This meaning is capable of being investigated. (4) There is a unity of biblical truth. (5) The importance of the comparative study of Scripture.

Third: The interpreter must begin his work by studying the grammatical sense of the text. To obtain this he has four sources: (1) the text itself: (2) the context; (3) parallel texts; (4) resources foreign to the text.

Fourth: A. Resources derived from the text.
    (1) The importance for the interpreter of knowing Hebrew and Greek.
    (2) But not absolutely necessary.
    (3) Importance of the Revised Version.
    (4) We must study the single words, (a) Not lay too much stress on etymological analysis. (6) Not seek for the ingenious and brilliant, but for the true, (c) Read the New Testament much, and constantly meditate, (d) Use best grammatical commentaries.
    (5) We must study the constructions, (a) Close relation between the language of the Old and New Testament.
    (6) Study the phrases and the nature of the discourse.

Fifth: B. Resources derived from the context.
(1) One of the most important means of finding the true meaning.
(2) Every book has a special object, especially in the New Testament. The Epistles of Paul.
(3) Many neglect the context (Dogmaticians).
(4) Sometimes too much importance is given to the context (Rationalists).

Sixth: C. Resources derived from Parallel Texts.

Seventh: D. Resources foreign to the text.
(1) The importance of a well-selected library.
(2) A careful choice must be made.
(3) Study only the works of the greatest ability.
(4) The true student must limit himself to a small number of books, at least in the beginning.
(5) A student cannot know the merit of a book until he has carefully studied it.
(6) The student should bear in mind that the object in study is to stimulate and enlighten his own mind, so that his further investigations may be reliable.
(7) Study the Bible first — then use other books.
(8) A list of valuable books for the English student of the Bible, which can be bought for about twenty dollars:
    1. A Teacher's Bible, containing Aids and Maps.
    2. The Revised Version
    3. A Dictionary of the Bible. (Peloubet, Schaff, Smith.)
    4. Commentary on the whole Bible. (Jamieson, Fausset, and Brown.)
    5. Student's Handbook of Topical Texts.
    6. Helps to the Study of the Bible.
    7. Young's Analytical Concordance.
    8. Angus' Bible Handbook.
    9. A Sacred History. (Kurtz, Smith, Blaikie.)
    10. Life of Christ. (Stalker Farrar, Geikie.)
    11. Life of Paul. (Stalker, Farrar. Conybeare and Howson.)

Eighth: To be able to interpret a book correctly, we must also take into consideration:

(1) The circumstances personal to an author. Moses, David, Amos, Isaiah, Ezekiel, John, Paul.

(2) The social circumstances of the author.

(3) The philological habits of authors.

(a) The orientals used highly colored language.

(b) The Jews were not a speculative people.

(c) No effort made in the direction of artistic writing, but the grand object of divine truth is to enkindle affections in the heart.

(4) The circumstances peculiar to the writings. These circumstances are both internal and external.

(a) Internal circumstances.

1. There is a difference in the nature of the writings, some being historical, others didactic, or oratorical, or parallelistic. (The word poetical conveys a wrong impression).

(b) External circumstances.

1. The persons to whom the writings are addressed will have an influence upon the writing. (The Epistle to the Romans).

2. The occasion of the writing will greatly help to a proper understanding of a book. (Galatians, II.Thess).

3. It is important for the interpreter to find out the object the writer has in view.

4. There is a general object of the whole book, and a special object in each division of a book.

5. The general object of each book, as well as the special objects in view, can only be found out by the attentive reading of a book, at one sitting.

6. Of great help is the comparative reading of the Bible, combined with meditation upon the successive details.

7. For the encouragement of those desiring to read a book at one sitting, the following facts are given:

First — Seventeen of the twenty-seven books of the New Testament can be carefully read in less than half an hour each.

Second — Five (Rom., I. Cor., II. Cor., Heb., Rev.) may be carefully read in an hour each.

Third — The historical books require from 1 to 2 hours each.

PART II.
The Grace of the Holy Spirit.

First: In the Old Testament the Spirit of God is especially described as working in the creation (Gen. 1: 12; Ps. 33: 6;) preservation (Ps. 104: 29, 30), and government of the material world.

Second: This is also assumed by Christ and his Apostles, though not directly asserted.

Third: In the New Testament the work of the Spirit is directly described in its immediate relation to our salvation.
> (1) He glorifies Christ, John 16: 14.
> (2) He bears witness of Christ, John 15: 26, 27.
> (3) He convicts the world of sin, John 16: 8.
> (4) He teaches men, II. Tim. 3: 16.
> (5) He guides believers into all truth, John 16: 13.
> (6) He helps our infirmities, Rom. 8: 26.
> (7) He bestows spiritual gifts, I. Cor. 12: 11.

Fourth: By the grace of the Holy Spirit we mean the relation and conduct of God towards man as a sinner, Eph. 1: 6, 7.

Fifth: It is repeatedly called the grace of God. II Thess. 1:12; Gal. 2: 21; I. Cor. 15: 10; II. Cor. 6: 1; Rom. 5: 15; Eph. 3: 2; Col. 1:6; Tit. 2: 11; Heb. 2- 9; 12:15.

Sixth: It is also called the grace of our Lord Jesus Christ. Gal. 1: 6; 6: 18; Rom. 16: 20; I. Cor. 16: 23; II. Cor. 8: 9; Phil. 4: 23; I. Tim. 1: 14; II. Pet. 3: 18.

Seventh: We speak of the grace of the Holy Spirit, because the Holy Spirit applies the gifts of grace and redemption to the heart of sinful man.

Eighth: He is the special gift promised by Christ. John 7: 39; 14:26; 15:26; 16.7; Acts 1:5.

Ninth: He works in believers as the Spirit of the Father and of Christ, John 16: 13-15.

Tenth: He is the divine ruling principle of the new life. Rom. 8:2-4; I. John 3: 24.

Eleventh: This grace of God has been especially manifested in the sending of the Son, and in His mediatorial work. John 1: 14, 16; Rom. 5: 20, 21; Eph. 2: 7.

Twelfth: By this grace we are saved through faith. Acts 15: 11; Rom. 3:28: 4: 16; Eph. 2- 8; Tit. 3: 7.

Thirteenth: In this grace and by this grace we stand. Rom. 5:2; I. Pet. 2: 10

Fourteenth: The grace of God is utterly opposed to works. Gal. 5:3. 4; Rom. 4: 4, 16; 6: 14, 15; 11: 6; John 1: 17.

Fifteenth: This grace is in most definite contrast to sin. Rom. 5: 20, 21; Eph. 1:7; 2: 3-5.

Sixteenth: The grace of God through the Word acts before conversion, in the act of conversion, and after conversion.

Seventeenth: For the sake of clearness, we may distinguish the acts of grace before conversion as follows:
>   (1) Prevenient grace, the implanting of the first Holy thought and godly desire.
>   (2) Preparative grace, which prepares the heart.
>   (3) Exciting grace, which works in the heart.

Eighteenth: In the act of conversion, which is brought about by the Holy Spirit by means of the Word, we may distinguish:
>   (1) Operating grace, which works (a) the knowledge of sin, and (b) compunction of heart.

(2) Completing grace, which works faith and confidence in Christ, which is the final act of conversion, and takes place instantaneously.

Nineteenth: After conversion we may speak of the grace of the Holy Spirit as:

(1) Co-operating grace, which works in man after his conversion, and preserves him in the faith, and assists and strengthens him.

(2) Indwelling grace, which dwells in the heart of man and changes it spiritually, enabling him to grow in grace and sanctification.

Twentieth: As the acts of applying grace follow one another in certain relations and connections, we may speak of "The Order of the Works of Grace." Acts 26:17, 18.

(1) The calling or vocation, I. Pet. 2:9.

(2) Illumination, II. Cor. 4:6.

(3) Regeneration, John 3:3, 5.

(4) Conversion, Acts 26:20.

   (a) Repentance, Acts 2:38.

   (b) Faith, Rom. 10:8-11.

(5) Justification, Rom. 3:24, 25.

(6) Mystical union with God, John 15:1-5.

(7) Renovation and sanctification, Eph. 4:22-24; I. Thess. 5: 23, 24.

STUDY IV.
PART I.
The Inspiration of the Bible.

First: The importance of this question.

Second: False views held by many at the present day.
    (1) Natural inspiration, identifying inspiration with genius.
    (2) Universal Christian inspiration, identifying it with the illumination common to every believer.
    (3) Partial or Essential inspiration, the view so popular at the present day, the watchword of which is "The Bible contains the word of God."
    (4) The Illumination theory, maintaining that there are different degrees of inspiration, and that the Bible is not equally inspired. (Superintendence, elevation, direction, suggestion).
    (5) Mechanical inspiration, ignoring the human altogether making the writers but mechanical instruments.

Third: This question is not one of theory, but of facts. The Bible alone can decide which is the true view.

Fourth: The Bible itself testifies that it is the word of God in the language of men, truly divine, and, at the same time, truly human.

Fifth: This view, that the Bible is the word of God, and that all parts of it are equally inspired, is known by the name of Plenary or Full inspiration.

Sixth: We must carefully distinguish between revelation, inspiration, and spiritual illumination.

(1) Revelation is that act of God by which he directly communicates truth, not known before, to the human mind.

(2) Inspiration is that act of God by which he preserved man from error in proclaiming the will of God by word of mouth, or in committing to writing the original Scriptures.

(3) Spiritual illumination refers to the influence of the Holy Ghost, common to all Christians.

(4) Not all that is in the Bible has been directly revealed to man. It contains history and the language of men; even of wicked men.

(5) But there is absolutely nothing in the Bible which is not inspired. The history recorded in the Bible is true; the language and deeds of good and evil men, even of Satan himself, though they may be evil, are faithfully recorded.

(6) The sacred writers were so guided and influenced by the Spirit, that they have been preserved from every error of fact and of doctrine. The history remains history; things not sanctioned by God, recorded in the Bible, are to be shunned (2 Tim. 3:10); nevertheless all these things were written under the guidance and influence of the Holy Spirit, and therefore inspired.

(7) Christians have never laid claim, when in the possession of sound reason, to divine inspiration, and to an authority like that of the Apostles. They expect and receive aid from the Holy Spirit, and this we call spiritual illumination, but not revelation and the gift of inspired teaching.

Seventh: If the Bible is not inspired, it has no authority.

Eighth: If the Bible is inspired it has authority.

Ninth: Without such an authority it cannot satisfy the three great wants of men:

(1) To give man a firm and well-grounded faith.

(2) To strengthen and raise feeble, sinful, irresolute, and suffering man.

(3) To prescribe a rule to regulate his conduct and govern his passions.

Tenth: The Scriptures expressly teach that they are inspired.

(1) No man can deny that Moses and the prophets profess to have received a mission from Heaven, for the purpose of transmitting to men a revelation from God.

(2) On the authority of the New Testament we can affirm:

(a) Christ promised the aid of the Holy Spirit to his Apostles. Matt. 10: 19, 20; Luke 21: 14, 15; John 14: 16, 20; 15:26; 16:7, 13, 14.

(b) He promised this aid as an extraordinary and special gift intended for the special times of the primitive Church. John 15: 26, 27; 16: 12-15.

(c) This was fulfilled in an extraordinary and special manner on the day of Pentecost. Acts 2.

(d) These extraordinary and special gifts of the Holy Spirit were either given directly to the fellow-laborers of the Apostles, or transmitted to them by the Apostles themselves. I. Cor. 12: 4-11, 28; Rom. 12: 4-6; Eph. 4:11, 12; I. Tim. 4: 14.

(3) The writers of the New Testament declare plainly and boldly that they were inspired. No one can ask proof more positive than is given in Gal. 1: 11, 12; Acts 15: 28; Eph. 3: 3-5; I. Thess. 2: 13.

(4) This claim of the sacred writers of the Old and New Testaments to a real inspiration, and to an authority which flows from it, was admitted by their contemporaries and successors.

Eleventh: For an able discussion of this whole subject, and of the equally important one of Interpretation of the Bible, see the "Biblical Hermeneutics" of Elliott and Harsha, a full outline of which is given in my "Theological Encyclopaedia," Part I. Exegetical Theology (pp. 123-155).

PART II.
The Calling or Vocation.

First: The Call is that act of grace by which the Holy Spirit, through the external preaching of the Word, makes known God's gracious will of salvation to those who are not members of His Kingdom. Acts 26:17; Rom. 10:13-15.

Second: In contradistinction to this direct call, we may also speak of an indirect call, through conscience and the natural knowledge of God. Rom. 1:19, 20; 2:14, 15; Acts 14:17; 17:27.

Third: God is earnest and sincere in his call. Matt. 23:37; I. Tim. 2:4; II. Pet. 3:9; Luke 14:23; Ezek. 18:23, 32; 33:11.

Fourth: The teaching of Jesus is very explicit.
(1) The call is unto sinners. Matt. 9:13; Luke 5:32; 19:10.
(2) Unto the weary and heavy laden. Matt. 11:28.
(3) The parable of the great supper. Luke 14:12-24.
(4) The parable of the marriage of the king's son. Matt. 22:1-14.

Fifth: The teaching of the Apostles.
(1) God has called us out of darkness. I. Pet. 2:9
(2) To inherit a blessing. I. Pet. 3:9.
(3) Unto his eternal glory in Christ. I. Pet. 5:10.
(4) According to his purpose. Rom. 8:28.
(5) Into the fellowship of His Son Jesus Christ our Lord. I. Cor. 1:9.
(6) In peace. I. Cor. 7: 15; Col. 3:15.
(7) In the grace of Christ. Gal. 1:6, 15.
(8) For freedom. Gal. 5:13.
(9) In the one hope of our calling. Eph. 4:1, 4.
(10) Into His own Kingdom and glory. I. Thess. 2:12.

(11) In sanctification. I. Thess. 4:7.
(12) Unto life eternal. I. Tim. 6:12.

Sixth: This call is the power of God unto salvation, able to effect regeneration and conversion, if not resisted by the perverse will of man. Rom. 1:16.

Seventh: This call is rejected by many. Matt. 22:14; Luke 14:18; Acts 13:46; Rom. 10:16, 21.

Eighth: A rejection of the call brings about a hardening of the heart. John 12:40; II. Cor. 2:15, 16.

Ninth: This call is to become universal. Matt. 28:19, 20; Mark 16:15; Luke 24:47. Whose fault is it that the Gospel is not made known to all men?

Tenth: The instrumental cause, by which the call is given, is the preaching of the Word. II. Thess. 2:14; Rom. 10:17.

Eleventh: The moving internal cause is the mercy and goodness of God, founded on the merit of Christ. II. Tim. 1:9.

Twelfth: The proclamation of the call is entrusted to the ministers of the Gospel. II. Cor. 5:20.

STUDY V.
PART I.
The Chronology and Geography of the New Testament.

First: The two eyes of history are chronology and geography.

Second: The chronology of the life of Christ. (Drill.)
Dec. 25, B.C. 5. Birth.
April, A.D. 8. The child Jesus in the Temple.
A.D. 8-26. The eighteen years retirement in Nazareth.
Feb., A.D. 27. The Temptation of Christ.
April, A.D. 27. At the first Passover. John 2: 13-25.
April, A D. 28. At the second Passover. John 5: 1-47.
April, A.D. 29. At the third Passover. John 6: 4.
Friday, April 7, A.D. 30. Crucifixion of Christ.
Sunday, April 9, A.D. 30. Resurrection.
Thursday, May 18, A D. 30. Ascension into Heaven.
(For fuller details see Harmony in Study VI.)

Third: The Chronology of the life of Paul. (Brill.) A.D. 1. Birth.
37. Conversion.
45. First Missionary Journey.
50. Council at Jerusalem.
50-54. Second Missionary Journey.
52. Writes I. and II. Thessalonians.
54-58. Third Missionary Journey.
57. Writes Gal., I. and II. Cor., Romans.
58. Arrested in Jerusalem.
59. In prison at Caesarea.
60. Voyage to Rome.
62. Writes Col., Eph., Philemon, Phil.
63. Released from prison. Writes Hebrews.

67. Writes I. Timothy and Titus.

68. Second captivity at Rome. Writes II. Timothy. Death.

Fourth: Other dates of sacred chronology.
44 A.D. Martyrdom of James, Acts 12: 1, 2.
60-70. Three Gospels and the Acts of the Apostles were written.
68. Martyrdom of Peter.
70. Destruction of Jerusalem.
90-100. John writes the Apocalypse, his Gospel, and three Epistles.
98-100. Death of John.

Fifth: Roman Emperors. (Drill.)
Augustus (27 B.C.-14 A.D.), Tiberius (14-37), Caligula (37-41).
Claudius (41-54), Nero (54-68), Galba (68), Otho and Vitellius (69),
Vespasian (69-79). Titus (79-81), Domitian (81-96), Nerva (96-98),
Trajan (98-117).

Sixth: The importance of being acquainted with the geography of the
New Testament world.

Seventh: Point out on the map the principal countries referred to in
the New Testament. (Drill.)
Libya, Egypt, Arabia, Palestine, Phoenicia, Syria, Mesopotamia, Asia
Minor, Thrace, Macedonia, Achaia or Greece, Illyricum, Italy.

Eighth: The principal seas. (Drill.)
Mediterranean, Black, iEgean, Adriatic, Sea of Galilee, Dead Sea.

Ninth: The principal Islands. (Drill.) Cyprus, Crete, Patmos, Sicily,
Melita or Malta.

Tenth: The provinces of Asia Minor. (Drill.) North: Bithynia,
Paphlagonia, Pontus. West: Mysia, Lydia, Caria. These three form
"the Asia" of Acts. South: Lycia, Pamphylia, Cilicia. Interior: Galatia,
Cappadocia, Lycaonia, Pisidia, Phrygia.

Eleventh: The provinces of Palestine. (Drill.) Judea, Samaria, Galilee,
Persea, Bashan.

Twelfth: Dimensions of Western Palestine. (Drill.)
(1) Area, 6,600 square miles (less than Massachusetts).
(2) From Dan to Beersheba, 180 miles; the coast line from Gaza to
Zidon, 180 miles; from Dan to the Mediterranean, about 25 miles;
from the Dead Sea to the Mediterranean, passing Gaza, 60 miles; the
valley of the Jordan from Dan to the Dead Sea, 134 miles.

Thirteenth: Natural divisions of Palestine. (Drill.)
> (1) The Maritime Plain, 8 to 20 miles wide.
> (2) The Shephelah, or foot-hills, 300 to 500 feet high.
> (3) The Mountain Region, from 2,500 to 4,000 feet high.
> (4) The Jordan Valley, a deep ravine, from 600 to 1000 feet
> below the level of the sea, and from 2 to 14 miles wide.
> (5) The Eastern Tableland.

Fourteenth: Locate the Mountains of Palestine. (Drill.) Lebanon,
Hermon, Tabor, Gilboa, Carmel, Ebal, Gerizim, Zion, Olives.

Fifteenth: Locate the principal Plains. (Drill.)
Phoenicia, Sharon, Philistia, Esdraelon, the Negeb, Jordan Valley, the
Hauran.

Sixteenth: Locate the principal Towns of Palestine. (Drill.) Gaza,
Joppa, Cresarea, Hebron, Bethlehem, Jerusalem, Bethel, Shechem,
Samaria, Nazareth, Cana, Jericho, Capernaum, Bethsaida, Dan.

Seventeenth: Locate the places mentioned in Paul's first Missionary
Journey (Acts 13: 1—14: 28). (Drill.) Antioch in Syria, Seleucia, Island
of Cyprus, Salamis, Paphos, Perga, Antioch in Pisidia, Iconium,
Lystra, Derbe, return to Perga, thence to Attalia, to Antioch.

Eighteenth: Locate the places mentioned in Paul's Second Missionary
Journey (Acts 15 : 36—18 : 22). (Drill.) Syria, Cilicia, Derbe, Lystra,
Phrygia, Galatia, Troas, Philippi, Amphipolis, Apollonia,
Thessalonica, Berea, Athens, Corinth, Cenchrea, Ephesus, Csesarea,
Jerusalem, Antioch.

Nineteenth: Locate the places mentioned in Paul's third Missionary
Journey (Acts 18: 23—21: 15). (Drill.) Antioch, Galatia, Phrygia,
Ephesus, Troas, Macedonia, Greece, Philippi, Troas, Assos, Mitylene,

Chios, Samos, Trogyllium, Miletus, Cos, Rhodes, Patara, Tyre, Ptolemais, Caesarea, Jerusalem.

Twentieth: Locate the places mentioned in Paul's voyage to Rome (Acts 27: 1—28: 16). (Drill.)
Caesarea, Sidon, Myra, Crete, Fair Havens, Melita or Malta, Syracuse, Rhegium, Puteoli, Appii Forum, Three Taverns, Rome. Twenty-first: The best work for the student to use is Hurlbut's "Manual of Biblical Geography."

PART II.
Illumination.

First: The natural man does not receive the things of the Spirit of God. I. Cor. 2:14.

Second: Because the mind of the flesh is enmity against God. Rom. 8:7.

Third: The wisdom of the world is opposed to saving knowledge. I. Cor. 1:20-25; II. Cor. 10:4, 5.

Fourth: The natural mind is darkened in understanding, and alienated from the life of God. Eph. 4:18; Acts 26: 18; II. Cor. 4:4.

Fifth: Illumination is that act of the Holy Spirit by which the intellect of man is enlightened.
    (1) With reference to his sinfulness and misery. Gal. 3:22.
    (2) With reference to the free grace of God in Christ. Eph. 1:18-20.

Sixth: Through the intellect, the will of man is also enlightened. Tit. 2:11-12.

Seventh: Paul prays that the Colossians may be enlightened, in order that they may lead a life of sanctification. Col. 1:9-10.

Eighth: We may distinguish between illumination and regeneration as follows:
    (1) Illumination refers more to the intellect; regeneration more to the will.

(2) Illumination consists rather in a knowledge of God's will, as revealed in His word; regeneration rather in the gift of faith and the implanting of a new life.

(3) Illumination prepares the way; regeneration follows.

Ninth: Illumination differs also from sanctification.

(1) By illumination we seek to make the intellect more perfect; by sanctification, the will.

(2) The effect of illumination is knowledge, Eph. 1:18; II. Cor. 4:6; the effect of sanctification is holiness and righteousness, Eph. 4: 24.

Tenth: The supernatural illumination of the Holy Spirit through the Word, can be resisted. II. Cor. 4: 3, 4.

Eleventh: The Holy Spirit enlightens us through the Word of God, heard, read, or meditated upon. II. Pet. 1: 18, 19.

Twelfth: The importance of committing Scripture to memory in our youth. The word of God, thus committed, always retains its illuminating power.

Thirteenth: Men are enlightened especially by the teaching and preaching of the word. Eph. 3:8, 9.

(1) Enlightening grace may also be called teaching grace. John 14: 26.

(2) As well as anointing grace, I. John 2:20, 27.

(3) It in fact opens the eyes of the mind. Acts 26:18.

(4) And takes away the veil which keeps out the light of the Gospel. II. Cor. 4:3, 4; John 5:35.

Fourteenth: There are three helps to spiritual illumination:

(1) Prayer. Eph. 1:17, 18; Col. 1.9; James 1:5.

(2) Meditation. John 5: 39; Acts 17: 11; Ps. 1. 1-3; 119: 97-100.

(3) Trials. Ps. 119:71, 72.

Fifteenth: Through the preaching of the law comes the knowledge of sin. Rom. 3:20; 7:7; Gal. 3:24.

Sixteenth: Through the Gospel we receive the knowledge of the grace of God in Christ. II. Cor. 4:4-6; 3:6-9.

Seventeenth: Ordinary illumination is progressive, the mind receiving continuously more and more light of the truth. II. Pet. 3:18; Col. 1:9, 10; Hosea 6:1-3.

Eighteenth: We may draw a distinction between literal and spiritual illumination.

(1) Literal illumination pertains to the external and intellectual knowledge of the doctrines of religion, and produces simply an historical assent to the Gospel, preparing the mind of the unregenerate to receive saving faith. II. Pet. 1:19; Eph. 3:9.

(2) Spiritual illumination is the work of the Holy Spirit in the mind of the truly regenerate, when the truth is not only known and admitted, but sealed by the internal testimony of the Spirit graciously dwelling in the heart. Eph. 1:17, 18; Col. 1:9-11; Phil. 1:9, 10; II. Pet. 1:11.

STUDY VI.
PART I.
Of a Harmony of the Four Gospels.

First: The first three Gospels are commonly called synoptical, because they each give to some extent a synopsis of Christ's life.

Second: The Gospel of John has very little in common with the first three Gospels, and is supplementary.

Third: A harmony has great practical value to the student.
    (1) It enables us to study the life of Christ in chronological order.
    (2) It enables us to compare the parallel accounts.
    (3) It gives vividness to the earthly life and teachings of Christ, enabling us to follow Christ from place to place.

Fourth: There are many difficulties in forming a harmony.

Fifth: Each Gospel contains something peculiar to itself, and each has something in common with the others. (See: Harmony).

Sixth: As Matthew writes for the evident purpose of proving that Jesus is the Messiah promised in the Old Testament, we need not expect a chronological biography, and only the earlier (Matt. 1:1—4:22) and later (Matt. 14: 1—28: 20) chapters of his Gospel have any chronological order. (See Harmony).

Seventh: Luke is mainly chronological, but a long passage (9:51—18:14), containing the history of about five of the last six months of Christ's ministry, is peculiar to Luke. (See Harmony).

Eighth: John alone gives us an account of the first year of Christ's ministry, and His Gospel, except the last four chapters, mainly consists of conversations of Christ, peculiar to John. (See Harmony.)

Ninth: Study carefully the seventy-eight questions given at the bottom of the harmony. (See Harmony).

The following chronological table of the Gospel History, exhibiting a harmony of the four Gospels, has been prepared with great pains, after a careful and repeated study of the most valuable works, both ancient and modern, which bear directly or indirectly on this important subject.

It is impossible to give, in this connection, the reasons for adopting this particular order in disputed passages. An attempt has also been made to indicate the places and the time when the events appear to have taken place. In this respect the writer is greatly indebted to the valuable works of Wieseler, Ebrard, Greswell, Andrews, Tischendorf, Robinson and Gardiner.

The best method of studying the Gospel History is by means of a harmony, and of the four Gospels, Mark deserves to be studied first, because it supplies the best basis for constructing a harmony, being written in chronological order. A harmony also furnishes the best analysis of a particular Gospel, and in the harmony here given, the analysis of the Gospel of Mark, being chronological, can be traced by the occurrence of the full face type.

HARMONY OF THE FOUR GOSPELS.	MATT.	MARK.	LUKE.	JOHN.

PART I.

EVENTS CONNECTED WITH THE BIRTH AND CHILDHOOD OF OUR LORD.

Time: About 13½ years. B. C. 6.—A. D. 8.

Sect.

	MATT.	MARK.	LUKE.	JOHN.
1. Preface..		1: 1	1: 1-4	1: 1-14
2. The Announcement of the Birth of John the Baptist. *Jerusalem. Autumn,* B. C. 6.			1: 5-25	
3. The Announcement of the Birth of Jesus. *Nazareth. Spring,* B. C. 5.			1: 26-38	
4. Mary visits Elizabeth................................ *Hill Country of Judæa. April—June,* B. C. 5.			1: 39-56	
5. Birth of John the Baptist. *Hill Country of Judæa. June,* B. C. 5.			1: 57-80	
6. The Birth of Jesus Christ......................... *Bethlehem. Dec. 25,* B. C. 5.	1: 18-25		2: 1-7	
7. The Genealogies of Jesus Christ...............	1: 1-17		3: 23-38	
8. An Angel announces the Birth to the Shepherds. *Near Bethlehem. Dec.,* B. C. 5.			2: 8-20	
9. The Circumcision and Presentation in the Temple. *Bethlehem and Jerusalem. Jan.-Feb.,* B. C. 4.			2: 21-38	
10. The Visit of the Wise Men...................... *Jerusalem and Bethlehem. Feb.,* B. C. 4.	2: 1-12			
11. The Flight into Egypt.............................. *Feb.,* B. C. 4.	2: 13-18			
12. The Return to Nazareth........................ *Spring.* B. C. 4.	2: 19-23		2: 39, 40	
13. The child Jesus in the Temple with the Doctors. *Jerusalem. Passover. April,* A. D. 8.			2: 41-50	
14. Christ's eighteen years' retirement in Nazareth. A. D. 8—A. D. 26.			2: 51, 52	

PART II.

FROM THE BEGINNING OF JOHN THE BAPTIST'S MINISTRY TO OUR LORD'S FIRST PASSOVER.

Time: About 9 months. Summer, A. D. 26—*April,* A. D. 27.

	MATT.	MARK.	LUKE.	JOHN.
15. The Preaching and Baptism of John. *The desert and the Jordan. Autumn,* A. D. 26.	3: 1-12	1: 2-8	3: 1-18	
16. The Baptism of Christ............................. *Bethany beyond Jordan. Jan.,* A. D. 27.	3: 13-17	1: 9-11	3: 21, 22	
17. The Temptation of Christ........................ *The desert beyond Jordan. Jan.—Feb.,* A. D. 27.	4: 1-11	1: 12, 13	4: 1 13	
18. The Testimony of John the Baptist........... *Bethany beyond Jordan. Feb.,* A. D. 27.				1: 15-34

Part I.—1. Into how many parts may the Gospel History be divided? 2 What does the first part comprise? 3. When and where was Christ born? 4. How much older was John the Baptist? 5. Give a brief account of the life of Christ to the age of twelve. 6. Describe the visit to Jerusalem. 7. How many years did Christ live in retirement? 8. Where? 9. What was His age at the end of this period?

Part II.—9. What period does the second part cover? 10. When and where did John the Baptist begin his ministry? 11. How old was Christ at his baptism? 12. How long was Christ tempted? 13. Mention all the events that occurred during the month of February, A. D. 27.

HARMONY OF THE FOUR GOSPELS.	MATT.	MARK.	LUKE.	JOHN.
19. The Calling of Andrew and Simon Peter...... *Near the Jordan, Feb.,* A. D. 27.	....	....	....	1: 35-42
20. The Calling of Philip and Nathanael............ *On the way to Galilee, Feb.,* A. D. 27.	....	... .	....	1: 43-51
21. The Marriage of Cana, and Departure to Capernaum. *Galilee, Feb.,* A. D. 27............	....	....	....	2: 1-12

PART III.

THE EVENTS OF THE FIRST YEAR OF OUR LORD'S MINISTRY.

Time: One year. Passover, April, A. D. 27 — *Passover, April,* A. D. 28. (780-781) *Year of Rome.*				
22. At the Passover, Christ purgeth the Temple .. *Jerusalem, April,* A. D. 27.	....	....	......	2: 13-25
23. The Conversation with Nicodemus............. *Jerusalem, April,* A. D. 27.	....	....	....	3: 1-21
24. Jesus baptizes by his disciples.............. *Judæa, Summer,* A. D. 27.	....	....	....	3: 22
25. Further testimony of John the Baptist......... *Ænon, near the Jordan. Autumn,* A. D 27.	....	....	....	3: 23-36
26. Christ's discourse with the woman of Samaria. *Shechem or Sychar, Dec.,* A. D. 27.	....	....	....	4: 1-42
27. The Healing of the Nobleman's Son........... *Cana of Galilee. Probably, Jan.,* A. D. 28.	....	....	....	4: 43-54

PART IV.

THE EVENTS OF THE SECOND YEAR OF OUR LORD'S MINISTRY.

Time: One year. Passover, April, A.D. 28 — *Passover, April,* A. D. 29. (781-782) *Year of Rome.*				
28. Our Lord's second Passover, and the Miracle at the Pool of Bethesda. *Jerusalem, April,* A.D. 28.	....	....	....	5: 1-47
29. The Imprisonment of John the Baptist......... *April,* A. D. 28.	....	....	3: 19, 20	
30. The Beginning of Christ's Ministry in Galilee. *April,* A. D. 28.	4: 12, 17	1: 14, 15	4: 14, 15	
31. Christ's preaching and rejection at Nazareth.. *April,* A. D. 28.	....	....	4: 16-30	
32. He fixes his abode at Capernaum, *April,* A.D. 28.	4: 13-16	....	4: 31, 32	
33. The Call of the first four Disciples. *Sea of Galilee, near Capernaum, April — May,* A. D. 28.	4: 18-22	1: 16-20	5: 1-11	
34. The Cure of a Demoniac in the Synagogue at Capernaum. *May,* A. D. 28...............	....	1: 21-28	4: 33-37	

Part III.—14. What was the length of our Lord's ministry? 15. What time does the third part include? 16. What is the date of the first Passover in our Lord's ministry? the second? the third? the fourth? 17. Which Evangelist records the early Judean ministry of our Lord? 18. Did Christ himself baptize? *John* 4: 2. 19. Sketch the history of this period.

Part IV.—20. What period does the fourth part cover? 21. When was John the Baptist imprisoned? 22. How long had his ministry continued? 23. In what year of his ministry did Christ begin His labors in Galilee? 24. What city became the centre of His labors? 25. What distinctive title is given to it? *Matt.* 9: 1. 26. When and where were the first four disciples called? 27. Their names?

HARMONY OF THE FOUR GOSPELS.	MATT.	MARK.	LUKE.	JOHN.
35. The Healing of Peter's wife's mother, and many others. *Capernaum. The same Sabbath as last. May,* A. D. 28.	8 : 14-17	1 : 29-34	4 : 38-41	
36. Christ retires to pray, and preaches throughout Galilee. *May,* A. D. 28.	4 : 23, 24	1 : 35-39	4 : 42-44	
37. The Cleansing of a Leper. *In one of the cities of Galilee. May,* A. D. 28.	8 : 2-4	1 : 40-45	5 : 12-16	
38. The Healing of a Paralytic at Capernaum. *Summer,* A. D. 28.	9 : 1-8	2 : 1-12	5 : 17-26	
39. The Call and Feast of St. Matthew. *Capernaum. Summer,* A. D. 28.	9 : 9-13	2 : 13-17	5 : 27-32	
40. The Discourse about Fasting. *Galilee.* *Summer,* A. D. 28.	9 : 14-17	2 : 18-22	5 : 33-39	
41. The Disciples pluck Ears of Corn on the Sabbath. *Near Capernaum. After Pentecost,* *Summer,* A. D. 28.	12 : 1-8	2 : 23-28	6 : 1-5	
42. The Healing of a Man with a withered Hand. *Probably Capernaum. Midsummer,* A. D. 28.	12 : 9-13	3 : 1-5	6 : 6-10	
43. The Pharisees begin to plot against Jesus. *Probably Capernaum. Midsummer,* A. D. 28.	12 : 14	3 : 6	6 : 11	
44. Jesus withdraws to the Sea of Galilee, where he heals many. *Midsummer,* A.D. 28.	12 : 15-21	3 : 7-12		
45. He retires to the Mountain, and chooses his Twelve Apostles. *Near Capernaum.* *Midsummer,* A. D. 28.	10 : 2-4	3 : 13-19	6 : 12-16	
46. Multitudes follow him. *Near Capernaum.* *Midsummer,* A. D. 28.	4 : 25	....	6 : 17-19	
47. The Sermon on the Mount. *Near Capernaum.* *Midsummer,* A. D. 28.	5 : 1-7 : 29	....	6 : 20-49	
48. Christ's return to Capernaum, and the Anxiety of his Friends. *Midsummer,* A.D. 28	8 : 1	3 : 19-21	7 : 1	
49. The Healing of the Centurion's servant. *Capernaum. Midsummer,* A. D. 28.	8 : 5-13	....	7 : 2-10	
50. Jesus restores to life the only son of a widow. *At Nain. Midsummer,* A. D. 28.	....	....	7 : 11-17	
51. John the Baptist's Question. *Probably Capernaum. Midsummer,* A. D. 28.	11 : 2-6	....	7 : 18-23	
52. Christ's testimony concerning John the Baptist. *Probably Capernaum, Midsummer,* A.D. 28	11 : 7-19	....	7 : 24-35	
53. Jesus is anointed by a penitent woman. *Probably at Capernaum. Autumn,* A. D. 28.	....	....	7 : 36-50	
54. Christ continues his circuit in Galilee, with the Twelve. *Autumn,* A. D. 28	....	....	8 : 1-3	
55. The Accusation of casting out devils by Beelzebub. *Capernaum. Autumn,* A. D. 28.	12 : 22-30	3 : 22-27	11 : 14-23	
56. Blasphemy against the Holy Ghost. *Same place and time.*	12 : 31-37	3 : 28-30	12 : 10	
57. Seeking after a Sign. *Same place and time.....*	12 : 38-42	....	11 : 29-36	
58. The Return of the Unclean Spirit. *Same place and time.*	12 : 43-45	....	11 : 24-28	
59. Christ's Mother and Brethren come to Him. *Same place and time.......................*	12 : 46-50	3 : 31-35	8 : 19-21	
60. Parables. *By the Sea of Galilee and in Capernaum. Autumn,* A. D. 28.				

28. Who was the fifth disciple? 29. When were "*The Twelve*" chosen? 30. What Sermon was delivered on this occasion? 31. Where is it recorded? 32. What miracles were performed at Capernaum?

3

HARMONY OF THE FOUR GOSPELS.	MATT.	MARK.	LUKE.	JOHN.
a) The Parable of the Sower.........................	13: 1-9	4: 1-9	8: 4-8	
b) The Reason why Jesus used Parables....	13: 10-17	4: 10-13	8: 9, 10	
c) Explanation of the Parable of the Sower.	13: 18-23	4: 14-20	8: 11-15	
d) The Parable of a Candle under a Bushel.	....	4: 21-25	8: 16-18	
e) The Parable of the Seed growing Secretly..........................	....	4: 26-29		
f) The Parable of the Wheat and Tares.........	13: 24-30			
g) The Parable of the Mustard Seed............	13: 31,32	4: 30-32		
h) The Parable of the Leaven......................	13: 33			
i) Christ speaking in Parables...................	13: 34,35	4: 33,34		
k) Explanation of the Parable of the Wheat and Tares	13: 36-43			
l) The Parable of the Hidden Treasure...........	13: 44			
m) The Parable of the Pearl of Great Price......	13: 45,46			
n) The Parables of the Draw-net and the Householder......	13: 47-52			
61. The Stilling of the Tempest on the Sea of Galilee. *Autumn*, A. D. 28......................	8:18,23-7	4: 35-41	8: 22-25	
62. The Healing of the Gerasene Demoniacs. *The South-eastern Shore of the Sea of Galilee. Autumn A. D. 28.*	8: 28-34	5: 1-20	8: 26-39	
63. The Miracles of the Healing of the Woman with an issue of blood, and the Raising of the Daughter of Jairus. *Capernaum. Autumn, A. D. 28.*	9: 18-26	5: 21-43	8: 40-56	
64. The Healing of two Blind men. *Near Capernaum. Autumn, A. D. 28.*	9: 27-31			
65. The Healing of a Demoniac. *Same.............*	9: 32-34			
66. Christ teaches at Nazareth, and is rejected a second time. *Autumn*, A. D. 28....	13: 53-58	6: 1-6		
67. Christ teaches throughout Galilee. *Winter. Jan.-Feb.,* A. D. 29.	9: 35-38	6: 6		
68. The Sending forth of the Twelve Apostles *Same.*	10:1-11:1	6: 7-13	9: 1-6	
69. Herod's opinion of Christ. *March-April,* A. D. 29. *782 Year of Rome.*	14: 1, 2.	6: 14-16	9: 7-9	
70. Death of John the Baptist. *Castle of Machærus, on the east side of Jordan. March-April,* A. D. 29. *782 Year of Rome.*	14: 3-12	6: 17-29		
71. The Feeding of the Five Thousand. *North-east Coast of the Sea of Galilee. April,* A. D. 29.	14: 13-21	6: 30-44	9: 10-17	6: 1-15
72. Christ walks upon the Sea of Galilee. *April,* A. D. 29.	14: 22-33	6: 45-52	....	6: 16-21
73. He heals the sick at Gennesaret .... *April,* A. D. 29.	14: 34-36	6: 53-56		
74. The People follow Jesus to Capernaum......... *April,* A. D. 29.	....	....	....	6: 22-24
75. Christ's Discourse concerning the Bread of Life. *Capernaum. Near Passover, April,* A.D. 29.	....	....	....	6: 25-7: 1

33. Where did Christ speak many parables? 34. How often was Christ rejected at Nazareth? 35. When was John the Baptist beheaded?

HARMONY OF THE FOUR GOSPELS.	MATT.	MARK.	LUKE.	JOHN.

PART V.

THE EVENTS OF THE FIRST HALF OF THE THIRD YEAR OF OUR LORD'S MINISTRY.

Time, Six months. Passover, April, A. D. 29—Feast of Tabernacles, Oct., A. D. 29. 782 Year of Rome.

	MATT.	MARK.	LUKE.	JOHN.
76. Christ confutes the Scribes and Pharisees. *Capernaum. Summer, A. D. 29.*		15: 1-9	7: 1-13	
77. Defilement. *Same.*		15: 10-20	7: 14-23	
78. He heals the Daughter of a Syrophœnician Woman. *Land of Tyre and Sidon. Summer, A. D. 29.*		15: 21-28	7: 24-30	
79. The Healing of a Deaf and Dumb man, and many others. *Decapolis, near the Sea of Galilee. Summer, A. D. 29.*		15: 29-31	7: 31-37	
80. Christ feeds the Four Thousand. *Same*		15: 32-38	8: 1-9	
81. The Pharisees and Sadducees demand a sign from Heaven. *Magdala or Capernaum. Summer, A. D. 29.*		15: 39-16: 4	8: 10-12	
82. Warnings against the Pharisees and the Sadducees. *North-east coast of the Sea of Galilee. Summer, A. D. 29.*		16: 5-12	8: 13-21	
83. Christ heals a Blind man. *Bethsaida. Summer, A. D. 29.*			8: 22-26	
84. The Confession of Peter. *Region of Cæsarea Philippi. Summer, A. D. 29.*		16: 13-20	8: 27-30	9: 18-21
85. Christ foretells his Passion. *Same.*		16: 21	8: 31	9: 22
86. Rebuke of Peter. *Same.*		16: 22, 23	8: 32,33	
87. The Cross must be borne. *Same.*		16: 24-28	8:34-9:1	9: 23-27
88. The Transfiguration. *Region of Cæsarea Philippi. Probably on Mt. Hermon. Summer, A. D. 29.*		17: 1-9	9: 2-10	9: 28-36
89. The Question as to the Coming of Elijah. *Same.*		17: 10-13	9: 11-13	
90. The Healing of the Lunatic Child. *Region of Cæsarea Philippi. Summer, A. D. 29.*		17: 14-21	9: 14-29	9: 37-42
91. Our Lord again foretells his Death and Resurrection. *Galilee. Autumn, A. D. 29.*		17: 22, 23	9:30-32	9: 43-45
92. The Tribute Money. *Capernaum. Autumn, A. D. 29.*		17: 24-27		
93. Several discourses with the Disciples. *Capernaum. Autumn, A. D. 29.*				
(a) On the Greatest in the Kingdom of Heaven		18: 1-5	9: 33-37	9: 46-48
(b) On one Casting out Devils			9: 38-41	9: 49,50
(c) On Offences		18: 6-9	9:42-50	
(d) The Parable of the sheep gone astray		18: 10-14		
(e) The Treatment of an erring Brother		18: 15-18		
(f) The Blessing promised to United Prayer		18:19, 20		
(g) The Parable of the Unmerciful Servant		18: 21-35		

Part V.—36. Into how many parts can the last year of our Lord's ministry be divided? 37. What period does the fifth part cover? 38. Mention the countries which Christ visited during these six months? 39. What are the most important events that occurred during this period?

HARMONY OF THE FOUR GOSPELS.	MATT.	MARK.	LUKE.	JOHN.
PART VI.				
THE EVENTS FROM THE FEAST OF TABER-NACLES UNTIL OUR LORD'S FINAL ARRIVAL AT BETHANY.				
Time, about six months.				
Oct., A. D. 29—*April,* A. D. 30.				
94. Jesus goes up to the Feast of Tabernacles..... *Road to Jerusalem. Oct.,* A. D. 29.				7: 2-10
95. Jesus at the Feast................................. *Jerusalem. Oct.,* A. D. 29.				7: 11-52
96. The Woman taken in adultery................. *Jerusalem Oct.,* A. D. 29.				7:53-8:11
97. Christ teaches in the Temple. *Same.*.........				8: 12-59
98. The Healing of the man born blind............. *Same.*				9: 1-39
99. The Parable of the Good Shepherd............. *Same.*				9: 40- 10: 21
100. Our Lord's final Departure from Galilee..... *Galilee and Samaria. Nov.,* A. D. 29.			9: 51-56	
101. Warnings to certain who would follow Christ. *Same.*	8: 19-22		9: 57-62	
102. He sends out the Seventy Disciples......... *Probably Samaria, Nov.,* A. D. 29.			10: 1-11	
103. The Doom of the Impenitent Cities. *Same.*	11: 20-24		10: 12 16	
104. The Return of the Seventy...................... *Samaria and Perea. Nov — Dec.,* A. D. 29.			10: 17-20	
105. God's truth revealed to the Humble............. *Samaria, Nov.,* A. D. 29	11: 25-30		10: 21-24	
106. He journeys through Perea. *Nov.,* A. D. 29.	19: 1, 2	10: 1		
107. The Parable of the Good Samaritan............. *Probably Perea, Nov.,* A. D. 29.			10. 25-37	
108. The Disciples are again taught how to pray.. *Samaria or Perea, Nov.,* A. D. 29.			11: 1-13	
109. Jesus reproves the Pharisees................. *Probably Perea, Nov.—Dec.,* A. D. 29.			11: 37-54	
110. Exhortation to the Disciples. *Same.*			12: 1-12	
111. The Parable of the Rich Fool. *Same.*			12: 13-21	
112. Discourses. *Same.*			12: 22-59	
113. How to regard God's judgments. *Same.*			13: 1-5	
114. The Parable of the Barren Fig-tree. *Same.*			13: 6-9	
115. Christ heals an Infirm Woman. *Same*			13: 10-17	
116. Parables. *Same.*			13: 18-21	
117. Discourses on the Way to Jerusalem............. *Perea, Dec.,* A.D. 29.			13: 22-35	
118. He visits Mary and Martha...................... *Bethany, Dec.,* A. D. 29.			10: 38-42	
119. The Discourse of Jesus at the Feast of Dedication. *Jerusalem, Dec.,* A.D. 29..........				10: 22-39
120. Jesus retires again to Perea. *Bethany, beyond Jordan, Dec.,* A. D. 29.				10: 40-42
121. The Healing of the Man with the Dropsy..... *Perea, Dec.,* A. D. 29.			14: 1-6	

Part VI.—40. How long a period does the sixth part cover? 41. What feast did Christ attend in Oct., A. D. 29? 42. How long was this before His death? 43. Who gives us an account of the doings of Christ during these last months? 44. In what country did Christ now mainly labor?

HARMONY OF THE FOUR GOSPELS.	MATT.	MARK.	LUKE.	JOHN.
122. Christ teaches Humility. *Same*			14: 7-11	
123. The Parable of the Great Supper. *Same*			14: 12-24	
124. What is required of disciples. *Perea. Dec.,* A. D. 29.			14: 25-35	
125. Parables. *Same.*				
a) The Parable of the Lost Sheep			15: 1-7	
b) The Parable of the Lost Piece of Silver			15: 8-10	
c) The Parable of the Prodigal Son			15: 11-32	
d) The Parable of the Unjust Steward			16: 1-13	
e) The Rebuke of the Pharisees.			16: 14-17	
f) The Parable of the Rich Man and Lazarus.			16: 19-31	
126. Various Sayings of Christ. *Perea. Dec.,* A.D. 29				
a) On Offences			17: 1, 2	
b) On Forgiveness			17: 3, 4	
c) On Faith			17: 5, 6	
d) On Duty			17: 7-10	
127. The Raising of Lazarus. *Perea and Bethany. Jan.—Feb.,* A. D. 30.				11: 1-14
128. The Gathering of the Council of the Jews. *Jerusalem. Jan.—Feb.,* A. D. 30.				11: 45-53
129. Christ abides in Ephraim *Feb.—Mar.,* A. D. 30.				11: 54
130. He begins his last journey to Jerusalem. *The borders of Galilee and Samaria. Mar.,* A.D. 30			17: 11	
131. The Cleansing of the ten Lepers. *On the borders of Samaria. March,* A. D. 30.			17: 12-19	
132. Discourse upon the coming of the Kingdom of God. *Same.*			17: 20-37	
133. The Parable of the Unjust Judge. *Same*			18: 1-8	
134. The Parable of the Pharisee and Publican. *Same.*			18: 9-14	
135. On Divorce and Marriage. *Same*	19: 3-12	10: 2-12	16: 18	
136. Christ blesses little Children. *Same*	19: 13-15	10: 13-16	18: 15-17	
137. The Rich Young Man. *Same*	19: 16-22	10: 17-22	18: 18-23	
138. On Riches. *Same.*	19: 23-26	10: 23-27	18: 24-27	
139. The Reward of them that leave all for His sake. *Same*	19: 27-30	10: 28-31	18: 28-30	
140. The Parable of the Laborers in the Vineyard. *Same*	20: 1-16			
141. Our Lord again foretells his Death and Resurrection. *The Valley of the Jordan, near Jericho. March,* A. D. 30.	20: 17-19	10:32-34	18:31-34	
142. The Ambition of the Sons of Zebedee reproved. *Near Jericho. March,* A. D. 30.	20: 20-28	10:35-45		
143. The Healing of two Blind Men near Jericho. *March,* A. D. 30	20: 29-34	10:46-52	18:35-43	
144. The Visit to Zacchaeus. *Jericho. March,* A. D. 30.			19: 1-10	
145. The Parable of the Pounds. *Near Jerusalem. March,* A. D. 30.			19:11-28	
146. Christ arrives at Bethany, six days before the Passover. *Friday evening, Nizan 8th, March 31st,* A. D. 30.				11: 55- 12: 1

45. When was Lazarus raised from the dead? 46. When did Christ begin His last journey to Jerusalem?

47. When did Christ arrive at Bethany?

HARMONY OF THE FOUR GOSPELS.	MATT.	MARK.	LUKE.	JOHN.

PART VII.

THE EVENTS OF OUR LORD'S PASSION AND DEATH.

Time. Eight days. From Saturday, April 1, A. D. 30, Nizan 9—Sunday, April 9, A.D. 30, Nizan 17.
SATURDAY, APRIL 1, A. D. 30. NIZAN 9.
Sunset on Friday—Sunset on Saturday.

HARMONY OF THE FOUR GOSPELS.	MATT.	MARK.	LUKE.	JOHN.
147. The Jews come to Bethany to see Jesus and Lazarus. *Saturday (Sabbath) Afternoon and Evening.*				12: 9-11
SUNDAY, APRIL 2, A. D. 30. NIZAN 10. *Sunset on Saturday - Sunset on Sunday.*				
148. The Triumphal Entry into Jerusalem.	21: 1-11	11: 1-11	19: 29-44	12: 12-19
MONDAY, APRIL 3, A. D. 30. NIZAN 11. *Sunset on Sunday—Sunset on Monday.*				
149. The Cursing of the Barren Fig-tree.	21:18, 19	11: 12-14		
150. The Second Cleansing of the Temple.	21: 12-17	11: 15-19	19: 45-48 21:37, 38	
TUESDAY, APRIL 4, A. D. 30. NIZAN 12. *Sunset on Monday—Sunset on Tuesday.*				
151. The Withering of the Fig-tree and the Power of Prayer.	21: 20-22	11:20-26		
152. The Authority of Christ questioned.	21: 23-27	11:27-33	20: 1-8	
153. The Parable of the Two Sons.	21: 28-32			
154. The Parable of the Wicked Husbandmen	21: 33-46	12: 1-12	20: 9-19	
155. The Parable of the Wedding Garment.	22: 1-14			
156. Question as to paying Tribute to Cæsar.	22: 15-22	12:13-17	20: 20-26	
157. Reply to the Sadducees concerning the Resurrection.	22: 23-33	12:18-27	20: 27-39	
158. The First and Great Commandment	22: 34-40	12:28-34	20: 40	
159. How is Christ David's Son ?	22: 41-46	12:35-37	20: 41-44	
160. The Scribes and Pharisees condemned	23: 1-39	12:38-40	20: 45-47	
161. The Widow's Mite		12:41-44	21: 1-4	
162. Certain Greeks desire to see Jesus.				12: 20-36
163. The Unbelief of the Jews.				12: 37-50
164. The Prophecy of the Destruction of Jerusalem and the End of the World.	24: 1-51	13: 1-37	21: 5-36	
165. The Parable of the Ten Virgins.	25: 1-13			
166. The Parable of the Talents	25: 14-30			
167. The Description of the Last Judgment.	25: 31-46			
168. The Jews plot Christ's Death.	26: 1-5	14: 1, 2	22: 1, 2	
WEDNESDAY, APRIL 5, A. D. 30. NIZAN 13. *Sunset on Tuesday—Sunset on Wednesday.*				
169. The Anointing by Mary of Bethany. *Afternoon and Evening.*	26: 6-13	14: 3-9		12: 2-8
170. Judas agrees to betray Christ.	26: 14-16	14: 10,11	22: 3-6	
THURSDAY, APRIL 6, A. D. 30. NIZAN 14. *Sunset on Wednesday—Sunset on Thursday.*				
171. The Disciples sent to prepare the Passover.	26: 17-19	14: 12-16	22: 7-13	
172. Christ enters the City	26: 20	14: 17	22: 14	

48. How many days are included in the seventh part? 49. When did a Jewish day begin? 50. What occurred on Saturday, before Passion Week? 51. Describe the events of Palm Sunday. 52. Of Monday in Passion Week. 53. Where did Christ spend his nights? 54. Describe the events of Tuesday. 55. Where was Christ on Wednesday? 56. What occurred on that day?

HARMONY OF THE FOUR GOSPELS.	MATT	MARK.	LUKE.	JOHN.
FRIDAY, APRIL 7, A.D. 30. NIZAN 15. *Sunset on Thursday—Sunset on Friday.*				
173. Christ reproves the Ambition of the Disciples. *Thursday Evening. Nizan 15.*	....	....	22: 24-30	
174. He washes the Feet of the Disciples............ *Thursday Evening. Nizan 15.*	....	....	....	13: 1-20
175. **The Announcement of the Betrayal**........ *Thursday Evening.*	26: 21 25	14:18-21	22: 21-23	13: 21-26
176. Judas withdraws. *Thursday Evening*............	....	....	....	13: 27-30
177. The New Commandment. *Thursday Evening.*	....	....	....	13: 31-35
178. **The Institution of the Lord's Supper**...... *Thursday Evening.*	26: 26-29	14:22-25	22: 19, 20 22: 15-18	
179. **Peter's Denial foretold.** *Thursday Evening.*	26: 30-35	14:26-31	22:31-38	13: 36-38
180. Christ's Last Discourse. *Thursday Evening.*	....	....	....	14:1-16:33
181. Christ's Sacerdotal Prayer. *Thursday Evening*	....	....	....	17: 1-26
182. **Christ enters the Garden of Gethsemane.** *Thursday Evening, near midnight.*	26: 36	14: 32	22: 39, 40	18: 1, 2
183. **The Agony in Gethsemane.** *Early Friday morning, between midnight and one o'clock.*	26: 37-46	14:33-42	22:41-46	
184. **The Betrayal and Taking of Jesus**........ *Friday morn., probably between 1 and 2 o'clock.*	26: 47-56	14:43-52	22:47-53	18: 3-12
185. Christ is first taken before Annas............ *Early Friday Morning.*	....	....	....	18: 13,14, 24
186. **Jesus is taken before Caiaphas.**.......... *Early Friday Morning.*	26: 57-66	14:53-64	22: 54, 55	18: 19-23
187. **The Mocking of the Servants.** *Same*......	26: 67, 68	14: 65	22: 63-65	[25-27
188. **Peter's Denial and Repentance.** *Same*....	26: 69-75	14:66-72	22: 56-62	18:15-18,
189. **Jesus before the Council**.................... *Daybreak, Friday Morning.*	27: 1	15: 1	22: 66-71	
190. **The Sanhedrim lead Jesus to Pilate**....... *Daybreak, Friday Morning.*	27: 2 .	15: 1	23: 1	18: 28
191. Judas repents and hangs himself....	27: 3-10			
192. **Jesus before Pilate.** 6-7 A. M	27: 11-14	15: 2-5	23:2-5	18: 29-38
193. Pilate sends Jesus to Herod. 7-8 A.M.........	....	....	23: 6-12	
194. **Jesus again before Pilate.** 7-9 A.M	27: 15-26	15: 6-15	23: 13-25	18: 39, 40
195. **Jesus mocked by the Roman soldiers**..... *Friday Morning, 7-9 A.M.*	27:27-31	15:16-19	....	19:1 3
196. "Behold the Man.".....	....	....	....	19: 4-7
197. Pilate's last conversation with Jesus. 7-9 A.M.	....	....	....	19: 8-16
198. **The Crucifixion.** 9 A.M.—3 P.M...............	27:32-56	15:20-41	23:26-49	19: 17-37
199. **The Burial.** 4-6 P.M.........................	27: 57-61	15:42-47	23:50-56	19:38-42
SATURDAY, APRIL 8, A.D. 30. NIZAN 16. *Sunset on Friday—Sunset on Saturday. Sabbath.*				
200. The Watch at the Tomb............................	27:62-66			

PART VIII.

THE EVENTS FROM OUR LORD'S RESURRECTION TO HIS ASCENSION.

Time: 40 Days. From Sunday, April 9, Nizan 17,
—Thursday, May 18, A.D. 30. 783 Year of Rome.
201. The Resurrection

57. Describe the events of Thursday. 58. When did *Good Friday* begin, according to Jewish reckoning? 59. Give an account of all that happened on Thursday evening. 60. Where was Christ about midnight? 61. When did the betrayal take place? 62. Give an account of Christ's trial. 63. How long was Christ on the cross? 64. Give an account of his crucifixion. 65. Of his burial. 66. What occurred on Saturday after Christ's death?

HARMONY OF THE FOUR GOSPELS.	MATT.	MARK.	LUKE.	JOHN.
a) Mary Magdalene and the other women come to embalm Christ	28: 1,2	16 : 1-4	24: 1, 2	20: 1
b) Mary Magdalene runs to find Peter and John.				20: 2
c) The other women enter the Sepulchre.	28: 2-8	16 : 5-8	24: 3-8	
d) Peter and John come to the Sepulchre and then go away			24: 12	20: 3-10
e) Mary Magdalene comes the second time and our Lord makes his FIRST APPEARANCE		16 : 9		20: 11-17
f) Christ appears to the other women on their return from the Sepulchre. THE SECOND APPEARANCE.	28: 9,10			
g) The Disciples do not believe the Testimony of Mary Magdalene and the other women		16: 10,11	24: 9-11	20: 18
202. The Report of the Watch	28: 11-15			
203. Christ appears to Peter (1 Cor. 15: 5). THE THIRD APPEARANCE.			24: 34	
204. Christ appears to Two Disciples on their way to Emmaus. THE FOURTH APPEARANCE.		16: 12,13	24: 13-35	
205. He appears to the Apostles at Jerusalem, Thomas being absent. THE FIFTH APPEARANCE.		16: 14	24: 36-43	20: 19-25
206. He appears again, Thomas being present. THE SIXTH APPEARANCE.				20: 26-29
207. He appears to seven of them as they fish in the Sea of Galilee. THE SEVENTH APPEARANCE.				21 : 1-24
208. Christ appears to the Apostles on a mountain in Galilee (1 Cor. 15: 6). THE EIGHTH APPEARANCE.	28: 16-20	16:15-18		
209. The Ascension into Heaven. Thursday, May 18, A. D., 30. THE NINTH APPEARANCE.		16:19,20	24: 44-53	
210. Conclusion				20: 30, 31 21: 25

67. What is the last division of Christ's life? 68. Describe the events of that first Easter Day 69. How often did Christ appear on the day of his resurrection? 70. Describe these appearances. 71. How many appearances are recorded in the Gospels? 72. How often did Christ manifest himself visibly after his resurrection? *Ten times.* 73. What appearance is not recorded in the Gospels? 1 Cor. 15: 7.

GENERAL QUESTIONS.

74. How old was Christ when he was crucified? 75 What was the length of his ministry? 76. How may the Gospel History be divided? 77. How many Passovers occurred during Christ's ministry? 78. What is the best method of becoming acquainted with the facts of Christ's earthly life? *By studying the Gospel History by means of a Harmony.*

FIRST READING.—*The Gospel of St. Mark*; in sections that Mark omits, read the first Gospel that records the narrative. SECOND READING.—Take the Gospel of St. Mark as your guide, and read as before, but in *parallel* passages read Matthew. THIRD READING.—As before, but in *parallel* passages read St. Luke. FOURTH READING.—As before, but in *parallel* passages read St. John.

PART II.
Regeneration.

First: By our natural birth we are born in sin, members of the kingdom of the world, by nature children of wrath. John 3:6; Eph. 2:3; Ps. 51:5

Second: This corruption of the human heart requires a new birth, the implanting of a new life. John 3:7; Rom. 8:6-8.

Third: Because there can be no entrance into the Kingdom of God without this new birth. John 3:3; II. Cor. 5: 17.

Fourth: For as by our birth we become partakers of Adam's nature, and death reigned in us, Rom. 5:12, 17, so we must become partakers of the divine nature, II. Pet. 1:4 that we may have life, Rom. 5:17.

Fifth: This new birth is described in the New Testament as—
 (1) A being born or begotten of God. John 1: 13; I. John 3:9; 4:7; 5:1, 18.
 (2) A being born anew (or from above). John 3:3, 7.
 (3) A being born of water and the Spirit. John 3:5.
 (4) A being born of the Spirit. John 8:6, 7.
 (5) A being begotten again. I. Pet. 1:23.
 (6) A quickening, or making alive. Eph. 2:1, 5; Col. 2:13.
 (7) A new creation. Gal. 6:15; II. Cor. 5:17.
 (8) A spiritual resurrection from the dead. Rom. 6:4-6; Eph. 2:1, 5; Col. 2: 12, 13.
 (9) The new man, the inward man. Eph. 4:24; Rom. 7:22; II. Cor. 4:16.
 (10) A washing of regeneration and renewing of the Holy Ghost. Tit. 3:5.

Sixth: We may distinguish between Regeneration, or the New Birth, in its stricter sense, and in its wider sense.

(1) In its stricter sense, as we here use it, regeneration refers to the beginning of the new life, the new birth proper, that act of God by which He implants in man the spiritual power to believe in Christ and thus to begin a spiritual life. In this strict sense it precedes faith proper, and produces faith in man that he may attain justification, renovation, sanctification, and eternal salvation. John 1:13; I. John 5:1; Tit. 3:5, 6.

(2) In its broader sense, it includes justification, renovation, and sanctification, and refers to the spiritual life in general. This latter is the popular usage of the word, as when we speak of "a regenerated man," *i.e.*, one who is a true Christian.

Seventh: We here use the word in its stricter and narrow meaning as the beginning of the new life, the first implanting of life in the mind, as the new birth, and in this sense regeneration is that act of the Holy Spirit by which God produces faith in us.

Eighth: Before regeneration, the intellect and will of man are —

(1) In darkness. Eph. 5:8; John 1:5.

(2) Incapable of receiving the things of the Spirit of God. I. Cor. 2:14.

(3) At enmity against God. Rom. 8:7.

Ninth: After regeneration the intellect and will of man are —

(1) In the light. Eph. 5:9.

(2) Capable of spiritually knowing the glory of God. II. Cor. 4:6.

(3) Alive unto God in Christ Jesus. Rom. 6:11.

Tenth: Regeneration, or the new birth, is effected by the Holy Spirit through the Word. James 1:18; I. Pet. 1:23; I. Cor. 4:15.

Eleventh: Scripture also speaks of regeneration in connection with Baptism. Rom. 6:3-6; Col. 2:12; Tit. 3:5, 6; John 3:5, 6.

Twelfth: The action of the Holy Spirit in implanting the new life can be resisted. Acts 18:5, 6.

Thirteenth: The grace of regeneration may be lost. I. Tim. 1:19.

STUDY VII.
PART I.
The Gospel According to Matthew.

First: The meaning of Gospel or *Evangelion.*

Second: We have but one Gospel of Jesus Christ, but according to four inspired Evangelists.

Third: At first, in addition to the Old Testament, Christians had only the oral teaching of the Apostles.

Fourth: It was their great aim to prove that Jesus was the Christ of prophecy. Acts 5: 42; 6:4.

Fifth: This oral teaching gradually received a fixed form.

Sixth: It is this "Oral Gospel" which underlies as a common source, the first three Gospels.

Seventh: The Gospel, according to Matthew, is based upon his own oral Gospel.

Eighth: The Gospel, according to Mark, is based on the oral Gospel of Peter.

Ninth: The Gospel, according to Luke, is based on the oral Gospel of Paul.

Tenth: The four Gospels have their separate characteristics.
    (1) Matthew presents our Lord to us mainly as the promised Messiah of the Old Testament.
    (2) Mark, mainly as the King of the world.

(3) Luke, as the Savior of sinners.

(4) John, as the true God-Man.

Eleventh: The author of the first Gospel is the Apostle Matthew.

> (1) Of Matthew's life we know very little.
>
> (2) His name is mentioned only on three occasions.
>
> > (a) At the time of his call, Matt. 9: 9-13.
> >
> > (b) In the list of the Apostles, Matt. 10: 2-4.
> >
> > (c) As present in that "upper chamber" after the ascension, Acts 1:13.
>
> (3) His Jewish name, which evidently was changed to Matthew when he became a disciple, was Levi. Mark 2: 14; Luke 5:27.
>
> (4) Matthew = Theodore = Gift of God. His father's name was Alphraus (Mark 2: 14), and before his call Matthew had been a tax-gatherer, Matt. 9: 9; Mark 2: 14; "the publican," Matt. 10:3.
>
> (5) Of his later history we have no trustworthy information.

Twelfth: The testimony of the early church is unanimous that Matthew wrote his Gospel for the Jewish Christians of Palestine.

Thirteenth: The Gospel was evidently written between 55 A. D. and 65 A.D.

> (1) It was written before the destruction of Jerusalem, Matt. 24: 15-20.
>
> (2) And a long time, at least some thirty years, after the death of Christ, Matt. 27: 8; 28: 11-15.

Fourteenth: All ancient authorities agree that Matthew wrote his Gospel in Palestine.

Fifteenth: The unanimous testimony of all antiquity is that Matthew wrote his Gospel in Hebrew, *i.e.*, in Aramaic, the vernacular dialect of Palestine.

Sixteenth: And yet these same writers all equally agree in accepting the Greek Gospel as we have it now, as the work of Matthew.

Seventeenth: The true solution is that Matthew wrote his Gospel in both the languages current at the time in Palestine, for the Greek is not a translation from a Hebrew original.

Eighteenth: For a close analysis of the Gospel, and in how far the Gospel is chronological, see the Harmony given in Study VI.

Nineteenth: For practical purposes the following analysis will suffice:
    (1) The birth and childhood of Jesus. Matt, 1: 1—2: 23.
    (2) The preparatory ministry of John the Baptist. Matt. 3: 1-12.
    (3) The baptism of Jesus, and his inauguration into his ministry. Matt. 3: 13-17.
    (4) His temptation. Matt. 4: 1-11.
    (5) His life and labors in Galilee and its neighborhood. Matt. 4:12— 18:35.
    (6) His departure from Galilee and journey to Jerusalem. Matt. 19:120:34.
    (7) His arrival at Jerusalem, betrayal, death and burial. Matt. 21:1— 27:66.
    (8) His resurrection. Matt. 28: 1-20.

Twentieth: Westcott gives us an excellent analysis, setting forth the scope and aim of Matthew's Gospel. (Abridged).
    (1) Introduction. Matt. 1:1—2 : 23.
    (2) The Prelude. Matt. 3: 1—4: 25.
        (a) The Baptist. Matt. 3: 1-17.
        (b) The Messiah. Matt. 4:1-25.
    (3) The Law-giver and Prophet. Matt. 5: 1—13: 52.
        (a) The new law in relation to the old. Matt. 5: 1—7: 29.
        (b) The testimony of signs. Matt. 8: 1—9: 34.
        (c) The commission. Matt. 9 : 35—11 : 30.
        (d) The contrast. Matt. 12: 1-50.
        (e) Parables of the Kingdom, its rise, growth, consummation. Matt. 13:1-52.
    (4) The King. Matt. 14: 1—25:46.
        (a) The character of the King. Matt. 14: 1—16: 20.
        (b) Glimpses of the Kingdom. Matt. 16: 21—20: 16.
        (c) The King claims his heritage. Matt. 20: 17— 25: 46.
    (5) Death, the Gate of the Eternal Kingdom. Matt. 26: 1—28: 20.

(a) The Passion. Matt. 26: 1—27: 66.
(b) The Triumph. Matt. 28: 1-20.

Twenty-first: Best methods of studying the Gospels.

(1) Read the whole Gospel at one sitting, and test the analysis of Westcott. (Matthew can be carefully read in two hours.) Repeat such a reading at least once a month. First week, Matthew; second week, Mark (can be read in one and a quarter hours); third week, Luke (two and a quarter hours); fourth week, John (one and three-quarter hours). Continue such a course of reading for years until you are perfectly familiar with the Gospel History.

(2) Read a second time, make an analysis of each chapter, and study the contents so thoroughly that you can give the outlines of each chapter.

(3) Review often, until you can give contents of any chapter from memory. Test yourself on chapters taken at random, as 3, 10, 13, 18, 21, 24, 25.

(4) Use the harmony continually, and always fix the time and locate the place.

(5) Read in regular order some good handy commentary, as Carr on Matthew, in the Cambridge Bible for Schools and Collegea.

PART II.
Conversion.

First: In the Scriptures conversion is spoken of in a two-fold sense:

(1) In its strict or special sense it is that act of grace by which the Holy Spirit subdues and breaks the stubborn will and hard heart of the sinner, and excites in him sincere grief for his sins by the Law, and enkindles true faith by the Gospel.

(2) In its broader sense it is regarded as the personal act of man, the result of God's work in his heart, the penitence and faith by which the sinner is said to convert himself, to turn away from sin unto God. Acts 3:19.

Second: On the one hand, conversion is spoken of in Scripture as a work of grace. Acts 11:21, 23.

(1) As wrought by God. Phil. 1:6; 2:13; Eph. 1:19; 2:10; Acts 21:19.

(2) As a gift received of God. I. Cor. 4:7; I. Cor. 15:10.

(3) As given by God. Acts 11:18; II. Tim. 2:25.

(4) As given by Christ. Acts 3:26; 5:31; Rom. 15:18.

Third: On the other hand, a life of conversion is required of man as his personal act. Acts 3:19.

(1) Man is not to harden his heart. Heb. 4:7.

(2) He is exhorted to repent. Matt. 3:2; 4:17; Luke 13:3; Acts 2:38; 8:22; 26:20.

Fourth: Both these Scriptural statements are in harmony.

(1) It is God who begins the work. John 6:44.

(2) The hearing of the Word makes the heart burn. Luke 24:32.

(3) The Word arouses the heart. Acts 2:37.

(4) The Lord opens the heart. Acts 16:14.

(5) Man can reject this grace. Matt. 23:37; John 5:40.

(6) By grace man can receive the Word, believe and keep it. John 17:6,8.

Fifth: Conversion consists of two parts, repentance and faith. Mark 1:15.

Sixth: It begins with repentance and is finished in faith. Acts 2:38.

Seventh: It is the work of the law to bring about that knowledge of our sinfulness and misery which leads to repentance. II. Cor. 7:10.

Eighth: It is the work of the Gospel to bring salvation, Rom. 1:16.

Ninth: Though the conversion of a man may be spoken of as an event taking place at a certain definite time, nevertheless we must daily lead a life of conversion, — daily repent and daily believe.

Tenth: The unregenerate and unconverted man cannot bring about his own conversion by his own strength or will, because it is the Word of God which effects this conversion. I. Cor. 2:14; Rom. 10:14, 17.

Eleventh: This conversion is effected by the Holy Spirit, through the supernatural power of the Word.
> (1) Through it God manifests the exceeding greatness of His power. Eph. 1:18, 19.
> (2) Through it God worketh in us, both to will and work His good pleasure. Phil. 2:13.
> (3) Through it God delivers us out of the power of darkness, and translates us into the Kingdom of His Son. Col. 1:12, 13.
> (4) Through faith in His Word we are made alive. Col. 2:12-13.

Twelfth: Not only is the beginning of man's conversion ascribed to God the Holy Spirit, but it is God who also consummates and perfects the good that He begins in us.
> (1) God who begins a good work will also perfect it. Phil. 1:6.
> (2) We are not to resist God, who worketh in us. Phil. 2:13.
> (3) We are not to grieve the Holy Spirit. Eph. 4:30.
> (4) We are not to quench the Spirit. I. Thess. 5:19.

(5) We are guarded through faith by the power of God unto salvation. I. Pet. 1:5.

(6) The God of all grace shall perfect, establish and strengthen believers. I. Pet. 5:10.

Thirteenth: Encouragement for leading sinners to a conversion.

(1) There is joy in heaven. Luke 15:7.

(2) With God. Ezek. 18:23; Luke 15:32.

(3) Among the saints. Acts 15:3; Gal. 1:23, 24.

(4) There is a great reward. Dan. 2:3.

(5) A soul shall be saved from death. James 5:19, 20.

STUDY VIII.
PART I.
The Birth of Christ the Fulfilment of Prophecy.

First: Christ was to be born of a woman. Gen. 3: 15; Isa. 9: 6, 7; Gal 4: 4.

Second: Of a virgin. Isa. 7: 14; Matt. 1: 18.

Third: Of the seed of Abraham. Gen. 12: 3; 18:18; 22:18; Gal. 3:16; Matt. 1:1.

Fourth: Of the seed of Isaac. Gen. 21: 12; 26:4; Heb. 11: 17-19; Matt. 1:2.

Fifth: Of the seed of David. Ps. 89: 3, 4, 29, 36; 132: 11; Isa. 11: 1-3; Jer. 23: 5; 33: 15; Acts 13: 23; Rom. 1: 3; Matt. 1: 1.

Sixth: The time when he was to appear. Gen. 49: 10; Num. 24:17; Dan. 9:24, 25; Hag. 2: 6, 7; Mai. 3: 1; Luke 2: 1.

Seventh: The place of his birth. Micah 5: 2; Matt. 2: 1; Luke 2: 4-6,

Eighth: A messenger shall go before him. Isa. 40: 3-5; Mal. 3:1; 4:5; Matt. 3: 1-3; Luke 1:17.

Ninth: His name was to be called Immanuel. Isa. 7: 14; Matt. 1:22, 23.

Tenth: He was to be adored by wise men. Ps. 72: 10, 15; Isa. 60:3, 6; Matt. 2:1-11.

Eleventh: The name Messiah and Christ. Ps. 2: 2.

PART II.
Repentance.

First: Repentance is the first or negative side, while Faith is the last or positive side of conversion. Mark 1:15; Acts 20:21.

Second: Repentance was the burden of John the Baptist's message. Matt. 3:2, 8.

Third: With this same message our Savior began his blessed work. Matt. 4:17. Compare also Rev. 2:5, 16; 3-3.

Fourth: To awaken repentance was the aim of Christ's miracles. Matt. 11:20, 21.

Fifth: Christ commands that repentance unto remission of sins is always to be the great theme of preaching. Luke 24:47.

Sixth: Is the great theme of the preaching of the Apostles. Acts 2: 38; 3:19; 11:18; 17:30; 26:20.

Seventh: The starting point of repentance is the state of sin. Eph. 2:1-3.

Eighth: We may speak of eight separate acts in repentance.
    (1) A true knowledge of our sinfulness. I. John 1:8; James 3:2.
    (2) A sense of the divine anger against sin. Jer. 10:24; I. Cor. 6:9; Gal. 6:7.
    (3) Anguish and fear of conscience. Ps. 6:1; 38: 4, 6.
    (4) True humiliation before God. Ps. 51:4; Luke 15:21; 18:13.
    (5) Frank confession of sin. Ps. 51:3; 32: 5; I. John 1:9.

(6) Genuine sorrow on account of sin. II. Cor. 7:10; Matt. 26:75; Matt. 5:4.

(7) Serious hatred of sin, and loathing of one's sinfulness. Job. 42:6.

(8) Purpose of amendment. Ezek. 18:27, 28.

Ninth: Repentance is the gift of God. Acts 11:18; II. Tim. 2:25,

Tenth: We should be led to repentance:
(1) By the goodness of God. Rom. 2:4.
(2) By His long suffering. II. Pet. 3:9.
(3) By the chastisement of God. Rev. 3:19.

Eleventh: The marks of a true repentance are of a two-fold character:
(1) Internal, consisting of a change of mind. Luke 18:13; Col. 3:2; Heb. 12:1-2.
(2) External, a bringing forth of fruit worthy of repentance. Matt. 3:8; Luke 19:8, 9; I. Thess. 1:9; Isa. 1:16, 17; Acts 26:20.

Twelfth: Danger of neglecting repentance. Matt. 11:20-24; Luke 13:3, 5; Rev. 2:5, 16, 21.

Thirteenth: Note five important facts:
(1) Now is the time for repentance. II. Cor. 6:2; Heb. 4:9
(2) Without repentance there can be no forgiveness of sins. Acts 2:38; 3:19; 8:22.
(3) There are grades of contrition; the anguish is not the same in all.
(4) Forgiveness of one's sins does not depend on the quality or quantity of our contrition, but alone upon the merits of Christ.
(5) As we daily sin, so our repentance must be daily; we must lead a life of repentance and faith. Matt. 6:12; Luke 11:4.

STUDY IX.
PART I.

The Gospel According to Mark.

First: It is universally agreed that the second Gospel was composed by Mark.

Second: There is but one person in the New Testament by the name of Mark. The John Mark of Acts 12:12, 25; 15:37 is the same as the John of Acts 13:5, 13 and the Mark of Acts 15:39; Col. 4:10; Philemon 24; II. Tim. 4:11; I. Pet. 5:13.

Third: Of Mark's parentage we know very little. His mother's name was Mary (Acts 12: 12), and he was a cousin of Barnabas (Col. 4:10), and therefore on his mother's side, of the tribe of Levi (Acts 4:36).

Fourth: We may infer that Mark was converted by Peter. Acts 12:11, 12; I. Pet. 5:13.

Fifth: Of his later life, after 68 A.D. (II. Tim. 4: 11) we have no trustworthy account.

Sixth: It is the unanimous testimony of the Early Church that the Gospel of Mark has a close connection with the "Oral Gospel" preached by Peter.

Seventh: There are four instances where Peter is specially mentioned by Mark, while he is omitted by the other Evangelists. Mark 1:36; 11:21; 13:3; 16:7.

Eighth: Some have also thought that the Apostle was unwilling to record what might specially tend to his own honor. According to this view, it was the modesty of the Apostle which caused the omission of Peter's name in six places.

(1) Mark 7:17, compared with Matt. 15:15. (2) Mark 6:50, 51 with Matt. 14: 28-31. (3) Mark 9:33 with Matt. 17: 24-27. (4) Mark 8:29, 30 with Matt. 16:17-19. (5) Mark 14:13 with Luke 22:8. (6) Luke 22:31, 32.

Ninth: There are reasons for supposing that the Gospel of Mark not only is based upon the oral Gospel of Peter, but that it also exhibits the oral tradition of the official life of our Lord in its earliest extant form.

Tenth: The Gospel was written chiefly for Gentile Christians, and especially for the use of the church in Rome.
This can be seen from the fact —

(1) That words which would not be understood by Gentile readers are explained: Boanerges, Mark 3:17; Talitha cumi, 5: 41; Corban, 7:11; Bartimmun, 10:46; Abba, 14:36; Eloi, Eloi, lama sabachthani, 15:34; Gehenna, 9:43.

(2) Jewish usages are explained. Thus we are told of "the washing before meals," Mark 7:3, 4; that the Mount of Olives is "over against the temple," 13:3; that "they sacrificed the passover on the first day of unleavened bread," 14:12; that the preparation was "the day before the Sabbath," 15:42.

(3) Matters interesting chiefly to the Jews are omitted. The only quotation from the Old Testament is found in Mark 1:2, 3, taken from Mai. 3:1; Isa. 40:3; and in Mark 15: 28 (if this verse be genuine), from Isa. 53:12.

(4) Mark uses several Latin forms, which do not occur in the other Gospels. Speculator, "a soldier of his guard," 6:27; Xestes = sextarius = "pot," 7:4; quadrantes, "a farthing," 12:42; centurion, 15:39, 44, 45.

Eleventh: The Gospel, no doubt, was written between A.D. 63 and A.D. 70.

(1) It is not likely that Mark wrote his Gospel before Paul wrote his letter to the Colossians (A.D. 62), in which Mark is only spoken of as a relative of Barnabas. Col. 4:10.

(2) It was evidently written before the destruction of Jerusalem (Mark 13: 1-23).

Twelfth: The Gospel according to ancient tradition, was written at Rome, in the Greek language.

Thirteenth: Eminent educators maintain, that of the four Gospels, that of Mark deserves to be studied first in order of time.
    (1) It forms the best basis for forming a harmony.
    (2) It is chronological.

Fourteenth: For an exact and close analysis of the Gospel, see the Harmony given in Study VI. The analysis of Mark is given in heavy type, as it follows the chronological order, and lies at the basis of the Harmony.

Fifteenth: The following outline, abridged from Westcott, will convey a general idea of the construction of the Gospel.
    (1) The Preparation. Mark 1:1-13.
    (2) The work foreshown by Acts. Mark 1:14—2: 12.
        (a) The Call. Mark: 14-20.
        (b) Signs. Mark 1:21—2:12.
    (3) Outlines of teaching. Mark 2 : 13-4 : 34.
        (a) Traits of the new life. Mark 2:13—3:12.
        (b) The Kingdom of God and the world. Mark 3:13—4:34.
    (4) Signs. Mark 4:35— 5:43.
    (5) The issue: Unbelief. Mark 6:1-6.
    (6) The Foundations of the Kingdom. Mark 6:7— 13:37.
        (a) The mission of the Apostles. Mark 6:7—8: 33.
        (b) Glimpses of the Kingdom. Mark 8:34—10: 31.
        (c) The sovereignty claimed. Mark 10:32— 13:37.
    (7) The eternal Kingdom entered through the gate of Death. Mark 14:1—16:20.

Sixteenth: For best method of study see Study VII., Part I., Twenty-first statement.

Seventeenth: Study the outlines of each chapter so thoroughly that you can give contents of any chapter from memory.

Eighteenth: In studying this Gospel use the Harmony continually, and fix time and place.

Nineteenth: Read a good handy Commentary as that of Maclear on Mark, in the Cambridge Bible for Schools and Colleges.

PART II.
Faith.

First: Christ having obtained salvation for men, this salvation is preached unto men, and through the Gospel forgiveness of sin is offered. Luke 24:47; Acts 5:31; 10:43; 13:38, 39; 26:18.

Second: To become a partaker of salvation, all that is necessary is to appropriate to one's self the promises of the Gospel. Mark 1:15; Acts 16:30, 31; John 3:16.

Third: Faith consists of three elements.
    (1) A knowledge of the things to be believed.
        (a) A " beholding of the Son." John 6:40; 12:45.
        (b) A "knowing." John 6: 69; 17: 3, 7, 8; Gal.4:9; Eph. 4:18.
    (2) Assent, a believing that what the Scriptures say are certainly true.
        (a) A "receiving." John 3: 11, 12, 32, 33.
        (b) An assurance of things hoped for. Heb. 11:1; Rom. 4:18.
        (c) A conviction of the reality of things not seen. Heb. 11:1; II. Cor.5:7. (These last two, (b) and (c), often pass over into confidence.)
    (3) Confidence in Christ.
        (a) Apprehending Christ. John 1:12; Luke 8:13; Rom. 5:17; I. Tim. 1:15, 16.
        (b) Appropriating Christ. John 3: 16, 18, 36; 20: 28; Gal. 3:26; Phil. 1:21; Heb. 10:22.
        (c) A believing on Christ; a giving of one's self up to Christ. John 6:29, 35, 40; Acts 9: 42; 10:43; 11:17; 16:31; Rom. 10:11.
        (d) A personal coming to Christ. John 3:20, 21; 5:40; 6:35.

(e) A following after Christ. John 8:12; 10:3.

Fourth: These three parts of faith are referred to in John 14:10, 11, 12.

Fifth: The first two parts of faith refer to the intellect; confidence is the act of the will.

Sixth: Where there is true faith, all three elements must be present.

Seventh: Confidence is the principal part of faith.
> (1) Mere knowledge does not save.
> (2) A general assent or historical faith does not save. James 2:19.
> (3) There must be a special assent, in which the sinner applies the promises of the Gospel to himself individually.
> (4) The general and special assent of faith are united in I. Tim. 1:15, 16.
> (5) It is distinctly stated in Scripture that confidence is the chief part of faith. Matt. 9:22; 15:28; I. John 5:4, 13.
> (6) It can also be inferred from many other passages. Luke 8:50; Matt. 8:26; 14:31; Rom. 4:20, 21; 8:31-39; James 1:6.

Eighth: We may therefore distinguish between a general and a special faith.
> (1) A man has general faith when he believes all things to be true which are revealed in the Word of God.
> (2) A man has special or saving faith when he believes that on account of the satisfaction of Christ, God is reconciled, and for Christ's sake his sins are forgiven him (Rom. 3:24, 25), and he has firm confidence to trust in the salvation obtained by Christ.

Ninth: God (and Christ) is the ground of faith, the authority, whose word man believes. John 5:47; Acts 27:25; Rom. 4:3; Gal. 3:6.

Tenth: To this faith Jesus sought to lead those who believed on Him, because of the signs which he did. John 2:83; 3:2; 4:48, 50.

Eleventh: God (and Christ) is the contents of our faith.
> (1) We must believe that God is. Heb. 11: G; James 2:19.

(2) That Jesus is the Christ. John 8: 24; I. John 5:1.
(3) What significance this has for us. I. John 4: 15; John 1:29; 3:36; Acts 4:12.

Twelfth: Christ is the aim and object of faith. John 3:16, 18, 36; 6:40; Acts 10: 43.

Thirteenth : Our salvation depends upon this faith in Christ. John 3: 36; 8:24; 20:31; Acts 4: 12; Heb. 11:6.

Fourteenth: We receive according to our faith. Matt. 8:13; 9:22, 29; 15:28.

Fifteenth: To believe in Christ is to obey the will of God. I. John 3:23; 5: 1; John 6:29. Compare I. John 2:23; 5:10.

Sixteenth: God is the efficient cause of our faith. Phil. 1:29.
    (a) It is the gift of God. Eph. 2: 8; I. Cor. 12: 9.
    (b) It is the working of God. Col. 2:12.
    (c) It is of God in its beginning. Phil. 2:13.
    (d) In its increase. Mark 9:24; Luke 17:5.
    (e) In its completion. II. Thess. 1:11; Phil. 1:6; Heb. 12:2.

Seventeenth: The instrumental cause of faith is the preaching of the Word. Rom. 10:14, 17; Mark 16:15, 16; Rom. 16:25, 26; Col. 1:3-6; II. Cor. 4:6; John 17:20.

Eighteenth: The power and energy of faith are twofold—receptive and operative.
    (1) Receptive faith passively receives Christ and everything obtained by his merit. John 1:12; 17:8; Acts 10:43; Gal. 3:14; Rom. 5:17; Col. 2:6.
    (2) Operative faith manifests itself actively by works of love. Gal. 5:6; James 2:17.

Nineteenth: "Faith, so to speak, has two bands. One, which it extends upward to embrace Christ with all His benefits, and by this we are justified; the other, which it reaches downwards to perform the works of love and of the other virtues, and by this we prove the reality of faith, but are not thereby justified."

Twentieth: Every man can satisfy himself whether he has the true faith which justifies or not.

> (1) For the Spirit himself beareth witness with our spirit, that we are children of God. Rom. 8: 16; I. John 4: 13; 3:21.
> (2) Because we can examine and prove our faith. II. Cor. 13:5; II. Tim. 1:12; John 14:23.

Twenty-first: There are degrees of faith.

> (1) It may be weak. Mark 9:24; Luke 17:5.
> (2) It may be strong. Rom. 4:20, 21; Col. 1:23.
> (3) We are to abound in, II. Co- 8: 7.
> (4) We are to attain a fullness of faith. Heb. 10: 22; II. Tim. 1:12.

STUDY X.
PART I.

The Gospel According to Luke.

First: It is universally agreed that the third Gospel was composed by Luke, " the beloved physician " of Col. 4: 14; " the fellow-laborer" and faithful friend of Paul, Philemon 24; II. Tim. 4:11.

Second: From Col. 4: 11, 14 we may infer Luke was a Gentile.

Third: His conversion must have taken place before he joined Paul at Troas. Acts 16:11.

Fourth: We may infer that Luke remained at Philippi during the second and third missionary journey of Paul (51-58 A.D.) Acts 17:1.

Fifth: No doubt he was preaching the Gospel in Philippi and its neighborhood.

Sixth: Luke joined Paul again at Philippi at the end of Paul's third journey (Acts 20: 5, 6), in order to accompany him to Jerusalem.

Seventh: He was Paul's constant companion after this:
> (1) Sailed with him to Rome. Acts 27:1.
> (2) Was by his side during his first imprisonment. Col. 4:14; Philemon 24.
> (3) Was with him during his second imprisonment. II. Tim. 4:11 (68 A.D.).

Eighth: Of Luke's later life we have no trustworthy account.

Ninth: It is the unanimous testimony of the Early Church, that the Gospel of Luke is based upon the "Oral Gospel" preached by Paul.

Tenth: The Gospel was written before the Acts of the Apostles. Acts 1:1.

Eleventh: As the book of Acts was written about 63 A.D. (Acts 28:30, 31), the Gospel evidently was written about 58-60 A.D., probably during Paul's imprisonment at Caesarea. (54)

Twelfth: It has never been doubted that the Evangelist wrote his Gospel in Greek. The Greek used by Luke is the purest in the New Testament.

Thirteenth: From his quotations from the Old Testament it can be seen that he mainly used the Septuagint or Greek translation, instead of the Hebrew original.

Fourteenth: The purpose for which the Gospel was written is definitely stated in the Introduction. Luke 1:1-4.

Fifteenth: Through a Gentile convert he addresses other Gentiles.

Sixteenth: Of Theophilus (Luke 1: 4) little is known.
> (1) It is clear that he was not an inhabitant of Palestine. Luke 1:26; 4:31; 8:26; 23:51; 24:13.
> (2) Nor a Macedonian, Acts 16: 12; nor an Athenian, Acts 17:21; nor a Cretan, Acts 27:8, 12.
> (3) But evidently a native of Italy, and perhaps an inhabitant of Rome. Acts 28:12-15.

Seventeenth: The predominant character of Luke's Gospel is the offer of the Gospel to all, — the thought that Jesus is the Savior of sinners.

Eighteenth: For an exact and close analysis of the Gospel, see the Harmony given in Study VI.

Nineteenth: Note the following points as peculiar to Luke's Gospel:
> (1) The early history of John the Baptist. Luke 1:5-30.
> (2) Certain events connected with the birth and childhood of Jesus. Luke 2:8-52.

(3) The narrative of the labors of Christ after His final departure from Galilee, until He comes into the borders of Judea. Luke 9:51—18:14.

(4) Twelve of the most striking Parables. (Verify.)

Twentieth: The following outline, abridged from Westcott, will serve to explain the connection of the several parts:

(1) Introduction. Luke 1:1—2:52.

(2) The Preparation. Luke 3:1—4:13.

(3) The Announcement. Luke 4:14-44.

(4) The Future Church. Luke 5:1—9:43a

    (a) Its universality. Luke 5:1—6:11.

    (b) Its constitution. Luke 6:12—8:3.

    (c) Its development. Luke 8:4-56.

    (d) Its claims. Luke 9:1-43a.

(5) The Universal Church. The Rejection of the Jews foreshown. Luke 9:6-18:30.

    (a) Preparation. Luke 9:43-11:13.

    (b) Lessons of warning. Luke 11:11—13:9.

    (c) Lessons of progress. Luke 13:10—14:34.

    (d) Lessons of discipleship. Luke 11:25—17:16.

    (e) The coming end. Luke 17:11— 18:30.

(6) The Sovereignty claimed. Luke 18:81— 81:88.

    (a) The Journey. Luke 18:31—19:87.

    (b) The entry. Luke 19:28-48.

    (c) The conflict. Luke20:1-38.

(7) The Sovereignty gained by Death. Luke 22:1—24:53.

Twenty-first: For best method of Study, see Study VII, Part I, Twenty-first statement.

Twenty second: Study the outlines of each chapter so thoroughly that you can give contents of any chapter from memory.

Twenty-third: Oodet has written one of the best commentaries on this Gospel. Though based on the Greek text, and withal somewhat bulky, it can be used by the English student. Farrar or Lindsay are also good.

PART II.
Justification.

First: Justification does not signify to make righteous, but to declare, to reckon righteous. Gal. 3:6; Rom. 4:3; James 2:23; Gen. 15:5, 6.

Second: It is a judicial process.
>(1) A judgment is spoken of. Ps. 143:2.
>(2) A criminal. Rom. 3:19, 20.
>(3) The law is the accuser and plaintiff. Rom. 3:19; Acts 13:39; Gal. 2:16; 3:11; John 5:45.
>(4) Conscience concurs with the accusation of the law, and is the witness. Rom. 2:15.
>(5) The indictment is read. Col. 2: 14; Rom. 2:13; 3:20, 23; Gal. 2:16.
>(6) There is an advocate. I. John 2:1.
>(7) Justification is opposed to condemnation. Matt. 12:37; Rom. 5:16; Acts 13:38, 39; Rom. 8:33, 34.
>(8) There is an acquittal. Rom. 4:6-8; Ps. 32:1.

Third: Justification differs from regeneration and conversion.
>(1) Regeneration is the new birth, a real and internal change which takes place within man. See Study VI, Part II.
>(2) Conversion is that work of grace by which the sinner turns away from sin unto God, and begins with repentance and is finished in faith. See Study VII, Part II.
>(3) Justification is an act of God, taking place apart from man, by which God, for the sake of the merits of Christ, acquits and pronounces righteous the sinner who truly believes in Christ.

Fourth: Before justification the sinner is under the wrath of God. Eph. 2:3.
>(1) He is under sin. Rom. 3:9, 23; Gal. 3:22.

(2) His iniquities and trespasses are unforgiven. Rom. 4:7, 8; Eph. 1:7; II. Cor. 5:19.

(3) Spiritual death has overtaken him, which unchecked will lead to eternal death. I. John 3:14; John 5:24.

(4) The wrath of God abideth on such a one. John 3:36.

Fifth: After justification, the sinner's relation to God is changed.

(1) He is in a state of grace. Eph. 2:8; II. Tim. 1:9.

(2) He has passed out of death into life. John 5:24.

(3) His iniquities are forgiven. Rom. 4: 7.

(4) Righteousness is reckoned unto him. Rom. 4:5, 6; II. Cor. 5:21; Phil. 3:9.

Sixth: Justification therefore consists of two things:

(1) Remission of sins. Rom. 4:7, 8; 3, 25; Acts 13:38; I. John 2:10; Eph. 4:32; II. Cor. 5:19.

(2) The imputation of Christ's righteousness.

(a) There is a righteousness of God. Rom. 3:21, 22.

(b) Obtained by Jesus Christ. Rom. 3:25, 26; 5:8, 9.

(c) We can obtain this righteousness of God in Christ. II. Cor. 5:21; Rom. 1:16, 17; I. Cor. 1:30.

(d) A righteousness not mine own, but which is of God, through faith in Christ. Phil. 3:9; Rom. 3:9, 10; 4:5.

(e) But of this righteousness many are ignorant, Rom. 10:3.

Seventh: Christ obtained the forgiveness of our sins through His vicarious sufferings and death.

(1) Christ was made sin in our behalf. II. Cor. 5:21; Gal. 3:13; Rom. 8:3.

(2) He bore our sins in His body. I. Pet. 2:24; Heb. 9:28.

(3) On Him was laid our guilt and punishment. I. Pet. 2:24; Isa. 53:4, 6-8, 11.

(4) He made propitiation to the justice of God for our sins (for divine wrath is simply a manifestation of divine holiness, the most intense energy of the holy will of God, the zeal of His wounded love) Rom. 3:24, 25; I. John 2:2; 4:10; Eph. 5:2.

(5) He gave His life a ransom for us. Matt. 20: 28; I. Tim. 2:5, 6; Tit. 2:14; I. Pet. 1:18, 19.

(6) He opened the way of reconciliation between man and God. Rom. 5:8-11; II. Cor. 5:18, 19; Eph. 2:16; 5:2; Col. 1:20.

(7) He obtained our forgiveness by means of His blood shed for our sins. Acts 20:28; Rom. 3:25; 5:9; Eph. 1:7; 2:13; Col. 1:20; Heb. 9: 12, 14; 13:12,20; I. Pet. 1:19; I. John 1:7.

(8) We may say therefore that Christ obtained the forgiveness of our sins by His passive obedience.

Eighth: Christ obtained a righteousness for us by the most perfect fulfilment of the law.

(1) God sent forth His Son that He might redeem them which were under the law. Gal. 4: 4, 5.

(2) To obtain a righteousness for every one that believeth. Rom. 10: 4.

(3) To do the will of God. Heb. 10:7.

(4) To fulfill the law. Matt. 5:17; 3:15.

(5) Christ has made satisfaction to the law in all things, in order that His fulfilment and obedience might be imputed to us. II. Cor. 5:21; Rom. 8:3, 4; Phil. 3:9.

(6) This righteousness obtained by Christ is imputed to us through faith. Rom. 3:22, 25, 26; Rom. 1:16, 17; Phil. 3:9.

(7) We may say therefore that Christ obtained this righteousness of God, which is imputed to us (Phil. 3:9) through His active obedience.

Ninth: The impelling internal cause of our justification is the purely gratuitous grace of God. Rom. 3:24; 11: 6; Eph. 1:7; 2:8, 9; II. Tim. 1:9.

Tenth: The impelling external and meritorious cause is the active and passive obedience of Jesus Christ our Mediator. Rom. 3:24; II. Cor. 5:21.

Eleventh: When we say we are justified by faith, we simply mean that faith is the instrument or receptive means by which the salvation, offered in Christ Jesus, is received.

Twelfth: A saving faith is one which apprehends the merit of Christ. Rom. 3:25.

Thirteenth: We must distinguish between an imputed righteousness, which belongs to the topic of justification, and the righteousness of new obedience, or inherent righteousness, which belongs to the sphere of sanctification.

Fourteenth: We are justified before God, and saved by faith alone. Every question of works is altogether excluded from the doctrine of justification before God. Rom. 3: 28; Gal. 2:16; Rom. 5:4, 5; 11:6.

Fifteenth: Justification by faith alone is the central doctrine of Protestantism.

Sixteenth: As effects of justification we may mention:
    (1) Our mystical union with God. John 15: 4-6; Eph. 3: 17; Gal. 2: 20.
    (2) Adoption as Sons of God. Gal. 3: 26; Rom. 8: 14; I. John 3: 2.
    (3) Peace. Rom. 5: 1, 5.
    (4) Access to divine grace. Rom. 5:2; Eph. 2: 18; 3: 12.
    (5) Sanctification and eternal life. Rom. 6:22; Acts 26: 18.
Seventeenth: We may also speak of certain properties of justification:

Seventeenth: Aspects of justification:
    (1) It is instantaneous; not gradual or successive, like illumination or sanctification.
    (2) It is perfect. Our sins are completely forgiven; not almost, or only half, or only a certain number. They are either forgiven or unforgiven. I. John 1: 7; Rom. 8:1; John 5:24.
    (3) Assurance. Rom. 8:38, 39; Eph. 3: 12; Heb. 10:11
    (4) Is renewed daily; for we must daily repent of our sins, and be daily, continually justified.
    (5) The state of justification may be lost. John 15: 2; Heb. 6:5, 6; I. Tim. 4:1.
    (6) But it may be recovered. John 6: 37; Isa. 1:18; Luke 15:11-32.

STUDY XI.
PART I.
The Gospel According to John.

First: From a careful study of the Gospel we learn that, the writer was
> (1) A Jew. The style is Hebraistic, and the thought is Jewish. John 1:19-28; 4:9,25; 6:14,15; 19:36,37.
> (2) A native of Palestine. For the writer shows a most intimate knowledge of Palestine and of Jerusalem. John 1: 44; 3:23; 5:2; 8:20; 10:23.
> (3) An eye-witness of what he relates. John 1: 14, 39; 4:6; 6:5, 7; 19:35; 21:24.
> (4) The Apostle John. John 13: 23; 19: 26; 20: 2; 21:2, 7, 20,24.

Second: With this agrees the external testimony. Irenaeus (died 202), who was instructed by Polycarp, the pupil of St. John, assigns the fourth Gospel to the Apostle John.

Third: Modern criticism has vainly tried to deny the genuineness of this Gospel.

Fourth: Of the first thirty and the last fifty years of John's life, we have scarcely any trace.

Fifth: Scripture, however, furnishes us with some details of John's life.
> (1) He was the Son of Zebedee and Salome, Matt. 27: 56; Mark 15: 40; the brother of James the Martyr, Mark 3: 17; Acts 12: 1, 2.
> (2) His father was a fisherman, of considerable means and of some influence. We infer this on account of the mention of —
>> (a) "The hired servants." Mark 1: 20;
>> (b) Their mother's substance. Luke 8:3.

    (c) John's own house. John 19: 27.

    (d) The fact that John was known to the high priest. John 18: 15.

(3) John followed his father's occupation until his call as an Apostle. Matt. 4: 21, 22.

(4) The two brothers, James and John, were surnamed by our Lord, Boanerges, — sons of thunder, Mark 3: 17. This title refers to the vehemence, zeal and intensity, which marked their character. Mark 9: 38; Luke 9: 54; Mark 10:35-41.

(5) To John belongs the memorable distinction of being the disciple whom Jesus loved. John 19: 26.

(6) Together with Peter, John is the principal character of the earlier chapters of Acts. Acts 3: 1 — 8: 25.

(7) During the next fifteen years we hear nothing of him until the Council at Jerusalem, A.D. 50. Acts 15: 4, 22; Gal. 2:9.

(8) Scripture says nothing more of John's Apostolic labors.

(9) His special work from 50 to 70 A.D. may have been that of teaching and organizing the churches of Judea.

Sixth: Early tradition, however, unanimously points to Asia Minor, and to Ephesus in particular, as the scene of the later activity of John.

    (1) During his stay at Ephesus he was banished to the isle of Patmos, but the time is uncertain.

    (2) Was released from exile, returned to Ephesus, and lived to an extreme old age.

Seventh: It is the almost unanimous tradition of the Church that the Apostle wrote his Gospel in his extreme old age.

Eighth: The Apostle himself indicates the purpose he had in view in writing this Gospel. John 19: 35; 20: 30, 31.

Ninth: The special characteristic of this Gospel is simplicity of language, combined with profoundness of thought.

Tenth: For a full analysis see the Harmony given in Study

Eleventh : Note especially the following points in the Harmony :

    (1) With the exception of chapter 18 and 19: 17-42, John refers to very few events common to the Synoptists.

(2) John is the only Evangelist who refers to the events of the first year of our Lord's ministry.

(3) He omits almost entirely all reference to the events of the second and third years, concentrating everything in recording the conversations of Christ, especially during the Passion week.

Twelfth: Read the Gospel of John at one sitting (one and three-quarter hours), in the light of the following outline, abridged from Westcott:

1. The Prologue. John 1 : 1-18.
2. The Self-Revelation of Christ to the World. John 1 : 19—12: 50.
(1) The Proclamation. John 1 : 19— 4 : 54.
    (a) The testimony to Christ. John 1 : 19—2: 11.
    (b) The work of Christ. John 2: 12—4: 54.
(2) The Conflict. John 5: 1—12: 50.
    (a) The Prelude. John 5: 1- 6: 71.
        (aa) In Jerusalem. The Son and the Father. John 5: 1-47.
        (bb) In Galilee. Christ and men. John G: l-7i.
    (b) The great Controversy. John 7: 1— 12: 50.
        (aa) The Revelation of faith and unbelief. John 7: 1—10:42.
        (bb) The decisive judgment. John 11: 1—12: 50.
(3) The Self-Revelation of Christ to the Disciples. John 13: 1—21 : 25.
(1) The last ministry of love. John 13: 1—17: 26.
(2) The Victory through death. John 18: 1—20: 31.
(3) The Epilogue. John 21: 1-25.

Thirteenth: Make a special study of the following sections. Write out the thought as clearly and concisely as possible.
Draw up your analysis in tabular form:
(1) John 1:1-18.
    I.—The Word in his absolute, eternal Being (1: 1).
    II. — The Word in relation to creation (1 ; 3-18).
        1. The essential facts (1: 2-5).
        2. The historic manifestation of the Word (1: 6-13).
        3. The incarnation as apprehended by personal experience (1 : 14-18).
(2) John 3: 16-21.

1. The divine purpose in the Incarnation (3: 16, 17).
2. The actual result (3: 18, 19).
3. The cause of the result in man (3: 20, 21).

(3) John 5: 19-47.
    1. The nature and prerogatives of the Son —
        (a) In relation to the Father (5: 19-23).
        (b) In relation to men (5: 24-29).
    2. The witness to the Son (5: 31-40),
And the ground of unbelief (5: 41-47).

(4) John 6: 26-58.

(5) John 10: 1-18.

(6) John 13: 31—14: 31.
    1. Separation: its necessity and issue (13: 31-38).
    2. Christ and the Father (14: 1-11).
    3. Christ and the disciples (14: 12-21).
    4. The law and the progress of Revelation (14: 22-31).

(7) John 15: 1—16: 33:
    1. The living union (15: 1-10).
    2. The issues of union; the disciples and Christ (15:11-16).
    3. The issues of union; the disciples and the world (15: 17-27).
    4. The world and the Paraclete (16: 1-11).
    5. The Paraclete and the disciples (16: 12-15).
    6. Sorrow turned to joy (16: 16-24).
    7. After failure, victory (16: 25-33).

(8) John 17: 1-26:
    1. The Son and the Father (17: 1-5).
    2. The Son and His immediate disciples (17: 6-19).
    3. The Son and the Church (17: 20-26.)

Fourteenth: The analyses here given are after Westcott, and are to be filled out. They are to be taken as a guide for personal study.

Fifteenth: The best commentaries on John are those by Westcott, Godet, Luthardt, Plummer, Milligan and Moulton.

Sixteenth: We would especially recommend the following works, bearing on the Four Gospels, to the student of the English Bible.
    (1) A good Harmony (Gardiner, Robinson, Fuller).

(2) A life of Christ (Stalker, Geikie, Farrar, Edersheim, Ellicott).

(3) Westcott's "Introduction to the Study of the Gospels."

(4) Ebrard's Gospel History. (For advanced students).

(5) Trench on the Miracles.

(6) Trench on the Parables.

PART II.
The Mystical Union and Adoption.

First: As has already been stated, we may conceive of an order in the work of the Holy Spirit:
>(1) Calling.
>(2) Illumination.
>(3) Regeneration, or the implanting of the new life, that faith may be attained.
>(4) Conversion, which begins in repentance and ends in faith.
>(5) Justification, for we are justified by faith.
>(6) At the moment a man is justified, then at the same time he is mystically united to God, and adopted as a son of God.
>(7) And as an effect of justification, there follows now renovation and sanctification.

Second: Nevertheless regeneration, justification, and the mystical union so closely cohere that they cannot be separated in order of time, but are simultaneous.

Third: The mystical union does not consist simply of the gracious operation of the Holy Spirit in believers, John 14: 26; 16:13; Rom. 8:26.
Fourth: But it is a true, literal, and most intimate union with God and Christ.
>(1) Christ and the Father will come unto the believer, and make abode with him, John 14: 23.
>(2) The Holy Spirit abideth with us, and shall be in us, John 14:17.
>(3) Christ is in us, John 17:26; Rom. 8: 10; Col. 1:27.
>(4) Our fellowship is with the Father, and with his Son Jesus Christ, I. John 1:3.
>(5) Believers are in the Father and the Son, John 17:21; I. John 2:24.

(6) Believers are in Christ Jesus, Rom. 8:1; I. Cor. 1:30; Eph. 2:6; I. John 5:20.

(7) Christ liveth in me, Gal. 2:20.

Fifth: God dwells in the believer as in a consecrated temple, by his special presence.

(1) The believer is the temple of God, I. Cor. 3: 16.

(2) The temple of the Holy Ghost, I. Cor. 3: 17; 6: 19.

(3) We become partakers of the divine nature, II. Pet. 1: 4.

(4) We are united to Christ as the branch to the vine, John 15: 1, 4, 5.

(5) Our bodies are members of Christ, I. Cor. 6: 15; Eph. 5; 30.

(6) Christ dwells in the heart of believers, Eph. 3: 17; II. Cor. 6:16.

Sixth: This is a special union between the believer and God, and differs from the general union between God and man, Acts 17:27,28.

Seventh: This special union is:

(1) A gracious one, John 14: 23; 17: 11, 81.

(2) Tends to the glory of God, and therefore glorious, I. Cor. 15:28.

(3) A mystical union, Eph. 5:32; Gal. 3:27.

Eighth: We are exhorted to maintain this mystical union with Christ, John 15: 4; Col. 2: 7, 19.

Ninth: This union with Christ is maintained:

(1) By faith, Gal. 2:20; Eph. 3:17.

(2) By abiding in him, John 15: 4, 6.

(3) By his word abiding in us, I. John 2: 24; II. John 9; John 14:23.

(4) By keeping his commandments, I. John 3:24.

(5) By partaking of the Lord's Supper, I. Cor. 10: 16, 17; John 6:55, 56.

Tenth: It bestows great blessings:

(1) It promotes growth in grace, Eph. 4: 15, 16; Col. 2:19.

(2) It promotes holiness and fruitfulness, John 15: 4, 5; Rom.

8:10; I. John 3: 6.

(3) Christ's righteousness is continually imputed to the believer, II. Cor. 5:21; Phil. 3:9.

(4) The believer is always free from condemnation, Rom. 8:1.

(5) The believer can have boldness and does not dread the coming of Christ, I. John 2: 28.

Eleventh: When we are justified by faith, we are not only united to Christ, but also adopted as sons of God, Gal. 3: 26; 4:4, 5.

(1) As long as a man lives under the law, he is a bond-servant, Gal. 3:23; 4:1, 3.

(2) As a slave he has no part in the inheritance, Gal. 4: 7.

(3) By justifying faith, man passes from a state of slavery to a state of sonship, Gal. 3: 25, 26.

Twelfth: To be under the influence of the Spirit of God is an evidence of divine sonship, Rom. 8:14.

(1) The Spirit makes himself known as a Spirit, not of bondage, but of adoption as a son, Rom. 8:15.

(2) This divine sonship is inseparably bound up with an inheritance, Rom. 8:17.

(3) As a son, he has a legal title to the inheritance, Gal. 4:7.

Thirteenth: The Father's love now rests upon the believer, and he can have the trust and confidence of a child, crying, Abba, Father, Gal. 4:5.

Fourteenth: This adoption as sons has been secured by Jesus Christ, Eph. 1:5, 6.

(1) He redeemed us from the curse of the Law, Gal. 3:13; 4:5.

(2) And became our brother, John 20:17; Rom. 8:29.

(3) So we have the same Father, John 20: 17; II. Cor. 6: 18.

(4) And are therefore heirs of God, and joint-heirs with Christ, Rom. 8:17.

Fifteenth: By nature man is a child of wrath, Eph. 2:3; Rom. 9:26.

Sixteenth: By faith the believer is invested with the rights of Christ, who by nature is the Son of God, and thus the believer becomes by adoption a child, a son of God, Gal, 3: 26; Rom. 8:15-17.

Seventeenth: The divine sonship of Paul is the same as the "children of God," those "begotten of God," of which John speaks, John 1:12; 1 John 3:9, 10; 5: 1, 2.

Eighteenth: Special privileges belong to believers as adopted sons of God.

> (1) Freedom from a servile fear, Rom. 8:15; Gal. 4:7; I. John 4:18.
>
> (2) Bearing his name, I. John 3:1.
>
> (3) Being the objects of the Father's peculiar love, Rom. 5:9-11.
>
> (4) The guidance and indwelling of the Holy Ghost, Rom. 8:14; Gal. 4:5, 6.
>
> (5) Child-like confidence in God, Gal. 4:6; Rom. 8:15.
>
> (6) The certain inheritance of the riches of our Father's glory, as heirs of God, and joint-heirs with Christ, I. Cor. 8:21-23; Gal. 4:7; Rom. 8:17.

STUDY XII.
PART I.
The Acts of the Apostles.

First: There is a close relation between the Acts and the Gospel according to Luke. Acts 1:1, 2.

Second: All the evidence which goes to prove that Luke was the author of the third Gospel, is evidence also for his authorship of the Acts. See Study X., Part I.

Third: In the latter half of the book the writer sometimes speaks in the first person. Acts 16: 10-18; 20:5—21: 18; 27: 1—28: 16.

Fourth: The writer was not Silas (Acts 16: 19-40), nor Timothy (Acts 20: 4, 5).

Fifth: For the main facts of Luke's life, see Study X., Part I.

Sixth: The key to the date of the book is found in its abrupt ending, Acts 28: 30, 31, being written about 63 A.D.

Seventh: The object of the work is to furnish a summary history of the origin, growth and spread of the Christian Church, so far as it was effected by the instrumentality of Peter and Paul.

Eighth: The history of the Acts is authentic.
(1) It has sustained its credit under the severest test of modern criticism.
(2) There are many most remarkable incidental coincidences between the Acts and the Epistles of Paul.

(3) The style and thought of the speeches of Peter, James and Paul, contained in the Acts, agree with the style and thought of their respective Epistles.

(4) There is a most minute agreement with contemporary history.

Ninth: A careful reading of Acts at one sitting (3 hours) will show that it naturally divides itself into eight sections.

(1) Pentecost, with the events preceding it, (30 A.D.). Acts 1:1—2:47.

(2) Events relating to the progress of the Gospel in Judea and Samaria (30-40 A. D.). Acts 3 : 1—9 : 43.

(3) The conversion of Cornelius and the admission of the Gentiles (40-44 A.D.). Acts 10: 1—12: 25.

(4) The first missionary journey of Paul (45-50 A.D.). A.C1 13: 1—14:28.

(5) The Apostolic Council at Jerusalem (50 A.D.) Acts 15: 1 39

(6) The second missionary journey of Paul (50-54 A.D.). Acts 15:40—18:22.

(7) The third missionary journey of Paul, and his apprehension at Jerusalem (54-58 A.D .). Acts 18: 23—23: 30.

(8) His imprisonment at Cae3area, and voyage to Rome (58-60 A.D.). Acts 23: 31—28: 31.

Tenth: Review carefully the chronology and geography of the Acts of the Apostles as given in Study V., Part I.

Eleventh: Analyze and study carefully the whole book, so as to be able to give the contents of each chapter from memory.

Twelfth: Prepare a brief sketch of Peter's life after the Ascension of Christ, as recorded in Acts.

(1) The return of the eleven to Jerusalem, and the election of a successor to Judas, Acts 1 : 12-26.

(2) The events of the day of Pentecost, Acts 2: 1-47.

(3) The healing of a man lame from his birth, and the events connected with it, Acts 3: 1 — 4: 37.

(4) The events recorded in Acts 5: 1 — 6: 4.

(5) Peter and John sent to Samaria, Acts 8: 14-25.

(6) Peter at Lydda and Joppa, Acts 9: 32-43.

(7) The history of Peter and Cornelius, Acts 10: 1—11: 18.

(8) The imprisonment of Peter by Herod, and his deliverance, Acts 12: 1-19.

(9) Peter at the council in Jerusalem, Acts 15: 1-11.

(10) This the last notice of Peter in the Acts.

Thirteenth: Make a special study of the speeches of Peter
  (1) Of his three missionary sermons.
    (a) On the day of Pentecost, Acts 2: 14-40.
    (b) In the temple, Acts 3: 12-26.
    (c) Before heathens, in the house of Cornelius, Acts 10:28-48.
  (2) Of his shorter apologies before the Sanhedrim,
    (a) Acts 4: 8-12, 19, 20; Acts 5:29-32.
  (3) Of several utterances within the Church.
    (a) Prayers, Acts 1: 24, 25; 4: 24-30.
    (b) Brief addresses.
      1. On the election of an Apostle, 1: 16-22.
      2. On the sin of Ananias and Sapphira, Acts 5:3, 4, 8, 9.
      3. On the appointment of deacons, Acts 6: 2-4.
      4. To Simon Magus, Acts 8: 20-23.
      5. His defense in the case of Cornelius, Acts 11: 4-18.
      6. His address at the Apostolic Council in Jerusalem, Acts 15:7-17.

Fourteenth: Analyze these speeches very closely, and write out in tabular form what Peter teaches with reference to the following topics:
  (1) The light in which the death of Jesus is regarded.
  (2) The resurrection of Jesus.
  (3) Of his exaltation to the right hand of God.
  (4) Of his Person, as true God and true Man.
  (5) Of the effects of his death, or his saving work.
  (6) Of the salvation offered in him, and for whom?
  (7) The conditions of salvation.
  (8) Forgiveness of sin.
  (9) Change of heart.
  (10) Repentance.

(11) Faith.
(12) Of the Church.
(13) Of Baptism.
(14) Of the preaching of the Word.
(15) Of the Second Coming of Christ as Judge.

Fifteenth: Prepare a brief sketch of Paul's life, as recorded in Acts.
(1) His persecution of the saints, Acts 7: 58—8: 3.
(2) His conversion, Acts 9: 1-18. (Compare parallel accounts in Acts 22: 5-16; 26:12-23.)
(3) His preaching at Damascus, Acts 9:19-25, (On Acts 9:22, 23, compare Gal. 1: 11-17.)
(4) His arrival at Jerusalem, Acts 9: 26-30. (On Acts 9: 26 compare Gal. 1: 18-24.)
(5) Barnabas and Paul at Antioch, Acts 11: 22-30.
(6) For the rest of Paul's history as recorded in Acts, see analysis of book as given in this lesson.

Sixteenth: Make a special study of the speeches of Paul.
(1) His preaching at Damascus, Acts 9: 20, 22.
(2) His reproof of Elymas, the sorcerer, Acts 13: 10, 11.
(3) His missionary address in the synagogue at Antioch in Pisidia, Acts 13: 16-47.
(4) His address to the Gentile inhabitants of Lystra, Acts 14 15-17.
(5) Brief notices of various discourses. Acts 14: 22, 27; 15: 12; 16:31.
(6) The sermon on the Areopagus in Athens, Acts 17: 16-81.
(7) His farewell discourse to the elders of the Church, at Ephesus, delivered at Miletus, Acts 20: 18-35.
(8) His speeches in self-defense.
    (a) At Jerusalem.
        1. Before the people, Acts 22: 1-21.
        2. Before the Sanhedrim, Acts 23: 1-0.
    (b) In Caesarea.
        1. Before Felix, Acts 24: 10-21, 24.
        2. Before Festus and Agrippa, Acts 26: 1-29.
(9) His discourses to the Jews at Rome, Acts 28: 17-20; 28: 23-29.

Seventeenth: Analyze these speeches very closely, and write out in tabular form what Paul teaches with reference to the following topics:

> (1) Jesus is the Son of God, the Christ, the Lord, the Savior.
>
> (2) His Davidic descent, his death on the cross, his resurrection.
>
> (3) The source of salvation.
>
> (4) Salvation consists of forgiveness of sins.
>
> (5) Conditions of salvation.
>
> (6) Repentance and faith.
>
> (7) A coming judgment.

Eighteenth: Make a special study of the speech of Stephen, analyze carefully, and arrange results in a tabular form. (Acts 7:2-60.)

Nineteenth: Read carefully the book of Acts, and compare its teachings with the Apostles' Creed, and add to the references here given:

> (1) I believe, 16:31;
>
> (2) In God, the Father Almighty, maker of heaven and earth; 4:24; 17:24;
>
> (3) And in Jesus Christ, 3: 20; 2: 36;
>
> (4) His only Son, our Lord. 2: 36; 9: 20; 9- 17;
>
> (5) Who was conceived by the Holy Ghost, 10: 38;
>
> (6) Born of the Virgin Mary, suffered under Pontius Pilate, 1:14; 2:23; 13:28.
>
> (7) Was crucified, 2: 23, 3G; 4: 10;
>
> (8) Dead, and buried; 2: 24;
>
> (9) He descended into Hell, 2: 31;
>
> (10) The third day he rose from the dead, 2: 31; 4: 10;
>
> (11) He ascended into heaven, 1: 11; 2: 34;
>
> (12) And sitteth on the right hand of God the Father Almighty, 2:33;
>
> (13) From thence he shall come to judge the quick and the dead. 1:11; 10:42;
>
> (14) I believe in the Holy Ghost; 2: 4; 5: 3, 4;
>
> (15) The holy Christian Church, the communion of Saints; 2:39, 42, 47; 20:28;
>
> (16) The forgiveness of sins; 2: 38;
>
> (17) The resurrection of the body, 4: 2;

(18) And the life everlasting. 5: 20; 11: 18; 13: 46.

Twentieth: We would recommend the following works bearing on the Acts of the Apostles to the student of the English Bible:

(1) Lumby's Commentary in the Cambridge Bible for Schools and Colleges, or Howson and Spence in the "Revision Commentary."

(2) A life of Paul (Stalker, Conybeare and Howson, Farrar).

(3) Green's life of the Apostle Peter.

PART II.
Renovation and Sanctification.

First: It is not enough for a man to know that his sins are forgiven in Christ Jesus; he must also grow in grace and holiness. II. Pet. 3:18; 1:5-8; Rom. 6:22.

Second: All exhortations to a holy life take it for granted that we possess salvation in Christ Jesus. Rom. 6:22.

Third: This is illustrated by the argument of the Epistle to the Romans.
> (1) Being justified by faith, we are in a state of grace. Rom. 5:1, 2.
> (2) We who died to sin, how shall we any longer live therein? Rom. 6:1, 2.
> (3) The law hath no dominion over the believer, because he is joined to Christ, that he might bring forth fruit unto God. Rom. 7:4.
> (4) What the believer does not do on account of indwelling sin (Rom. 7:17, 22, 23), Christ has fulfilled in us, who are in Christ Jesus, and who walk not after the flesh, but after the Spirit. Rom. 8:1-4.

Fourth: If we live by the Spirit, we must also walk by the Spirit. Gal. 5:25.

Fifth: For they that are of Christ Jesus have crucified the flesh with the passions and the lusts thereof. Gal. 5: 24; II. Cor. 5:17.

Sixth: For we are God's workmanship, created in Christ Jesus for good works. Eph. 2:10.

Seventh: Love is to be made perfect in us. I. John 4: 16-19.

Eighth: The new life manifests itself in a two-fold manner, negatively as renovation, and positively as sanctification. Eph. 4:22-24; Col. 3:9, 10.

Ninth: Sin still dwells in the believer after regeneration and justification. Rom. 7:17, 20, 23; Gal. 5:16-18; Heb. 12:1, 2.

Tenth: Our renovation progresses from day to day, and is to be continued throughout life. II. Cor. 4:16; Eph. 4:16.
> (1) We are to die unto sin continually. I. Pet. 2: 24; Rom. 6:11.
> (2) We are not to let sin reign in our bodies. Rom. 6:12-14.
> (3) We are continually to present our bodies a living sacrifice. Rom. 12:1, 2.
> (4) The believer must daily deny himself, take up the cross, and follow Christ. Matt. 16: 24; Luke 14: 33.
> (5) We must mortify our members which are upon the earth. Col. 3:5-10.

Eleventh: Believers must also resist the world and its lusts. I. John 2: 15-17; Rom. 12: 2; Gal. 6: 14; James 4: 4.

Twelfth: And resist the devil. Eph. 6: 10, 11; I. Pet. 5: 8, 9.

Thirteenth: This gracious act of the Holy Spirit in man, by which the regenerated and justified believer puts off the old man and the dominion of sin, in order that he may be renewed in the image of God, may be called renovation.

Fourteenth: The positive side, the putting on the new man, the obtaining of inherent holiness of mind and heart, may be called sanctification. Eph. 4:24; Col. 3:10; Rom. 13:14; 6:19, 22.

Fifteenth: This thought is expressed in various ways in Scripture:
> (1) We are to grow up in all things into Christ. Eph. 4: 15, 16.
> (2) We are to be rooted and builded up in Christ. Col. 2: 6, 7.
> (3) Always abounding in the work of the Lord. I. Cor. 15: 53.
> (4) A putting on of special graces. Col. 3: 12-14.
> (5) To be holy in all manner of living. I. Pet. 1: 13-16.
> (6) A putting on the new man. Eph. 4: 23, 24; Col. 3: 10

(7) A putting on the Lord Jesus Christ. Rom. 13: 14.

(8) A transformation by the renewing of your mind. Rom. 12:2.

Sixteenth: This life of sanctification is to extend to everything. Col. 3: 17; I. Cor. 10:31; I. Pet. 2:5.

Seventeenth: The essence of the new life is Love. I. Cor. 13: 1-13.

(1) Which manifests itself in love to God. I. John 4: 19, 20.

(2) In love to fellow believers. I. John 4: 11-13; John 13: 34.

(3) In love to your neighbor. II. Pet. 1:7; Luke 10:27; Rom. 13:9.

Eighteenth: Love is the fulfilment of the law. Matt. 5:17; Rom. 13:10.

Nineteenth: He who wishes to see the Lord must possess the graces of love, peace and holiness. Heb. 12:14.

Twentieth: To be exact, therefore, we may say, renovation is the negative side, and sanctification the positive side, of the life striving after purification and holiness, but in popular language these terms are continually interchanged.

Twenty-first: We may distinguish between Regeneration, Justification and Sanctification as follows:

(1) Regeneration refers to the implanting of the new life, and produces faith.

(2) Justification refers to the change of our relation to God, and consists of the remissions of sins, and the imputation of Christ's righteousness.

(3) Sanctification has to do with inherent righteousness, with the reformation of the mind, will, and affections, with the restoring of the divine image to the soul.

(4) Both regeneration and justification are instantaneous; sanctification is progressive, increasing from day to day.

(5) Regeneration and justification do not admit of degrees, but sanctification does admit of degrees, because the inner man is renewed from day to day.

(6) Regeneration precedes justification, and justification precedes sanctification. Titus 3: 5-7.

STUDY XIII.
PART I.
The Epistle of James.

First: The writer designates himself as "a servant of God and of the Lord Jesus Christ." James 1: 1.

Second: There are three persons by the name of James mentioned in the New Testament:
(1) James, the son of Zebedee, the brother of John, one of the twelve Apostles.
(2) James, the son of Alphseus, another of the twelve, known also as James, the Less. Mark 15: 40.
(3) James, the Lord's brother (Gal. 1: 19; Mark 6: 3; Matt. 13:55), who was not one of the twelve (John 7: 5).

Third: It is James, the Lord's brother, who wrote the Epistle of James, who, after the resurrection (I. Cor. 15: 7), is found among the believers (Acts 1 : 14).

Fourth: It was James, the Lord's brother, who occupied the place of greatest importance among the disciples at Jerusalem.
> (1) It was to him that Peter sent the news of his release. Acts 12: 17.
> (2) It was James, the Lord's brother, who presided over the council of Jerusalem, 50 A.D. Acts 15: 13-21.
> (3) It is to this same James that Paul reports on his return to Jerusalem, just before his imprisonment. Acts 21: 18.

Fifth: From a careful study of the Epistle, with reference to the persons addressed, we learn —
> (1) That it was addressed to the twelve tribes which are of the Dispersion. James 1: 1.

(2) This evidently means the Jewish Christians dwelling beyond Palestine.

(3) James exhorts them as "beloved brethren," "brethren" (James 1:16, 19; 2:5; 2:1; 3:1,10; 5:7); as begotten by the word of truth (James 1: 18); as believers in Christ (James 2: 1).

(4) That the condition of affairs among the Jewish Christians is not a happy one.

> (a) They are subject to many trials and temptations. James 1:2, 12,
>
> (b) To changes in social positions. James 1 : 9.
>
> (c) They profess faith, but do not give evidence thereof by works. James 1: 19-27; 2. 14-26; 3: 13.
>
> (d) They draw a distinction between the rich and the poor. James 2: 1-13.
>
> (e) They are addicted to sins of the tongue (James 3: 1-12), jealousy and factions (James 3: 13-18), pleasure (James 4: 1-10), evil speaking (James 4: 11, 12), boasting and self- confidence (James 4: 13-17), oppression (James 5: 4).

Sixth: It is highly probable that the Epistle is one of the earliest in the New Testament, if not the earliest. (50 A.D.)

> (1) The language is based upon the sayings of Christ. James 1: 22, and Matt. 7: 21, 26; James 2: 5, and Luke 6: 20; James 5: 12, and Matt, 5: 37.
>
> (2) Christianity still appears as a movement entirely within Judaism.
>
> (3) The custom of anointing with oil, of which we hear nothing later, manifestly was still a trace of the practice of the Apostles. Compare James 5: 14 with Mark 6: 13.
>
> (4) The membership of the Church was still mainly of the poorer classes.
>
> (5) James does not antagonize the Pauline doctrine of justification, for throughout the whole epistle he attacks errors of life and not of doctrine. He does not in any way refer to the Pauline doctrine of justification.

Seventh: The Epistle was evidently written while James was at the head of the Church in Jerusalem, and being so well known and preeminent it was not necessary to distinguish himself from others of the same name. James 1:1.

Eighth: The fact that this Epistle was not unanimously accepted into the Canon until the third century, arises from the circumstance that it remained for a long time in the possession of exclusively Jewish-Christian circles.

Ninth: It is, however, already found in the Peshito, the Syriac version, at the close of the second century.

Tenth: Read the Epistle carefully and divide into sections with appropriate headings:

(1) James 1:1, Address and greeting.
(2) James 1: 2-12. Exhortations regarding the endurance of temptation.
(3) James 1 : 13-18. The nature of temptation.
(4) James 1: 19-27. Exhortations to be doers of the Word, and not hearers only.
(5) James 2: 1-13. Respect of persons inconsistent with the faith.
(6) James 2: 14-26. Saving faith will produce good works.
(7) James 3: 1-18. On the government of the tongue.
(8) James 4: 1-17. Various exhortations.
   (1) Against wars and fightings. James 4: 1-3.
   (2) Against lusts and worldly desires. James 4: 4-10.
   (3) Against evil speaking, James 4: 11-12.
   (4) Against ungodly and presumptuous confidence. James 4: 13-17.
(9) James 5: 1-6. Denunciation of woe on the rich in this world.
(10) James 5: 7-11. Exhortation to endure unto the coming of the Lord.
(11) James 5: 12-20. Various exhortations.

Eleventh: Study carefully each section, and write out the thought as clearly and concisely as possible.
Twelfth: This is eminently a practical Epistle.

Thirteenth: Study the Epistle as a whole, section by section, with reference to its practical truths.

    (1) Duty to God.

    (2) Duty to Man.

        (a) In the State.

        (b) In the Church.

        (c) In the Family.

    (3) Duty to Self.

PART II.
The Fruits of the Spirit, or Good Works.

First: The new life of the believer as growing in sanctification makes itself known by good works, Phil. 1:9-11.

Second: The works of the believer are called good, not because they are perfect, but because
    (1) They proceed from a good heart, Matt. 12: 35; I. Tim. 1:5;
    (2) And are in some degree conformed to the will of God, Rom. 12:2

Third: All good works have some imperfection.
    (1) They may still increase in perfection, Eph. 4:15.
    (2) And correspond more perfectly to the divine law, Rom. 7:14;
    (3) They lack in purity of motive, James 3:2;
    (4) For the flesh ever lusteth against the Spirit, Gal. 5:17.

Fourth: Good works have their origin in a true and living faith in Christ, Gal. 5:6.

Fifth: We cannot speak of the moral actions of the unconverted as "good works," Rom. 14:23; Matt. 7:18.

Sixth: These can only attain a civil righteousness, Rom. 2:14

Seventh: For good works are described in Scripture as:
    (1) The fruits of the Spirit, Gal. 5:22;
    (2) The fruit of the wisdom that is from above, James 3:17.
    (3) Fruits worthy of repentance, Matt. 3.8; Luke 3:8; Acts 26:20.
    (4) Performed through Jesus Christ, Phil. 1:11;

(5) Directed to the glory and praise of God, Phil. 1: 11; I. Cor.10:31;

(6) The fruit of those abiding in Christ, John 15:4, 5;

(7) Wrought by God in us, Phil. 2: 13;

(8) Proceeding from faith unfeigned, I. Tim. 1:5.

Eighth: Good works must be wrought by the regenerate, James 3:26.

(1) Not to justify us, Rom. 3: 28; Gal. 2: 16;

(2) Nor to earn salvation as a merit, Rom. 3: 24; Eph. 2: 8, 9;

(3) But to show our obedience to God, II. Pet. 1:8; Matt. 7:21;

(4) And prove the existence of faith, Gal. 5: 22, 23.

(5) And glorify the Father, John 15:8; Phil. 1:11;

(6) Because we have been created in Christ Jesus for good works, Eph. 2:10;

(7) Because being made free from sin, we have become servants of righteousness, Rom. 6:18, 22;

(8) Because God exhorts us, Col. 3: 12-14; II. Pet. 1 : 10, 11;

(a) To be rich and fruitful in good works, I. Tim. 6: 18; Col. 1:10.

(b) To be careful in maintaining good works, Tit. 3:8, 14.

(c) To be perfect in every good thing to do his will, Heb. 13:21.

(d) To provoke one another unto love and good works, Heb. 10:24.

(9) Because they are designed to lead others to glorify God, Matt. 5:16; I. Pet. 2:12.

Ninth: God "will render to every man according to his works, Rom. 2:6; II. Cor. 15:10.

(1) Believers shall be rewarded according to their works, I. Cor. 3:8; Rom. 2:7, 10; I. Cor. 15:58; Rev. 22:12; Matt. 16:27.

(2) The wicked shall be judged according to their works, II. Cor. 5:10; Rom. 2: 8, 9; II. Cor. 11:15; Rev. 2:23; 20:11, 13; II. Tim. 4:14.

Tenth: There are certain great principles underlying the doctrine of good works.

(1) The harvest depends on the seed sown, Gal. 6:7, 8.

(2) Upon the amount sown, II. Cor. 9:6;

(3) God is not unrighteous to forget our work and love, Heb. 6:10;

(4) Our labor is not in vain in the Lord, I. Cor. 15:58;

(5) To bring forth fruit unto God belongs to the full-grown and perfect man, I. Cor. 2:6; Heb. 15:14; James 3:2.

(6) This is the perfect man of which the Bible speaks, Phil. 3:15; Matt. 5:48;

(7) Not as though the Christian were at any time perfect in this life, and without sin, not needing to grow in grace and holiness, Phil. 3:12-16.

Eleventh: Seven suggestive tables:

(1) The three Christian Virtues: Faith, Hope, Love, I. Cor. 13: 13.

(2) The Four cardinal virtues: Prudence, Temperance, Fortitude, Justice.

(3) The seven Spiritual gifts: Wisdom, Understanding, Counsel, Strength, Knowledge, Godliness, Holy Fear. Isa. 11: 2.

(4) The twelve fruits of the Spirit: Love, Joy, Peace, Patience, Longsuffering, Mercy, Goodness, Meekness, Faith, Modesty, Chastity, Sobriety. Gal. 5: 22.

(5) The seven Spiritual works of Mercy.

    1. To instruct the ignorant.

    2. To correct offenders.

    3. To counsel the doubtful.

    4. To comfort the afflicted.

    5. To suffer injuries with patience.

    6. To forgive offenses and wrongs.

    7. To pray for others.

(6) The seven corporal works of mercy.

    1. To feed the hungry and give drink to the thirsty.

    2. To clothe the naked.

    3. To harbor the stranger and needy.

    4. To visit the sick.

    5. To minister unto prisoners and captives.

    6. To care for the orphan.

    7. To bury the dead.

(7) The Seven Deadly Sins and their contrary virtues:

    1. Pride— Humility.

2. Covetousness — Liberality.
3. Luxury — Chastity.
4. Envy — Gentleness.
5. Gluttony — Temperance.
6. Anger— Patience.
7. Sloth — Earnest serving of God.

Twelfth: Add the proper Scripture references to these tables.

STUDY XIV.
PART I.
The First Epistle of Peter.

First: It is unanimously held that this Epistle was written by the Apostle Peter. I. Pet. 1:1.

Second: It was universally accepted as genuine by the Early Church.

Third: The life of Peter before the Ascension of Christ.
(1) His name, Simon = Hearer, Peter = Cephas = Rock.
(2) His early home, Bethsaida (John 1:44); was married and removed to Capernaum (Matt. 8: 14).
(3) Held the first place among the Apostles.
(4) Trace his history as given in the Gospels by means of the Harmony, or an Index, or Concordance.
(5) After the Ascension, Peter assumes a position of special importance. See Study XII., Twelfth statement.
(6) Was accompanied by his wife in his missionary journeys. I. Cor. 9:5.
(7) Writes his first Epistle from Babylon, about 58-63 A.D.
(8) Suffered martyrdom at Rome about 67 A.D.

Fourth: Read the Epistle carefully, and note what references Peter makes to himself.
(1) He is an Apostle of Jesus Christ. I. Pet. 1: 1.
(2) A fellow-elder. I. Pet. 5: 1.
(3) A witness of the sufferings of Christ. I. Pet. 5: 1.
(4) A partaker of future glory. I. Pet. 5:1.
(5) Is in Babylon at the time of writing. I. Pet. 5: 13.
(6) His companions, Sylvanus and Mark. I. Pet. 5: 12, 13.

Fifth: Read the Epistle a second time, and note what we can learn about the persons addressed.

    (1) They are the elect saints. I. Pet. 1: 1, 5, 8; 2: 9.

    (2) Sojourners of the Dispersion in Asia Minor. I. Pet, 1: 1.

    (3) Mainly Jewish Christians. I. Pet. 1: 1, 16; 2: 6, 8; 3: 5, 6.

    (4) With many Gentiles. I. Pet. 1: 14, 18; 2: 10; 3: 6; 4: 3.

    (5) Undergoing grievous trials. I. Pet. 1:7; 4: 12, 13.

    (6) Spoken against as evil-doers. I. Pet. 2: 12; 3: 16.

Sixth: Evidently written between 58-63 A.D.

    (1) Peter seems to have known the Epistle to the Romans.

    (2) Seems to have written after the Epistle to the Galatians.

    (3) Seems to have written a few years before his martyrdom.

Seventh: Read the Epistle a third time and divide into sections. Write out appropriate headings.

Eighth: Study carefully each section; write out the thought as clearly and concisely as possible.

Ninth: Study the Epistle so thoroughly as to be able to give contents of each chapter from memory.

Tenth: This Epistle illustrates the Lord's Prayer in a remarkable way:

    Our— I. Pet. 1 : 4.

    Father— I. Pet. 1 : 3, 17.

    In Heaven— I. Pet. 1 : 4, 12.

    Hallowed be Thy name — I Pet. 1: 15, ">6.

    Thy Kingdom come — I. Pet. 2: 9.

    Thy will be done— I. Pet. 2. 15; 3: 17; 4: 2, 19.

    Daily bread — I. Pet. 5 : 7.

    Forgiveness of sins — I. Pet. 4: 1, 8.

    Temptation— I. Pet. 4: 12.

    Deliverance from evil — I. Pet. 4: 13.

    Kingdom— I. Pet. 5: 11.

    Power— I. Pet. 1:5; 4: 11.

    Glory— I. Pet. 1: 11, 21; 4: 11, 14; 5: 1, 10.

    Forever and ever — I. Pet. 4: 11; 5: 11.

    Amen— I. Pet. 4. 11; 5:11.

Eleventh: Study the first chapter and note all passages referring to the doctrine of the Trinity. Peter speaks of:

The Father. I. Pet. 1: 2, 3. 15, 17, 21, 23.

Christ. I. Pet. 1:1,2, 3, 7, 11, 13, 19.

The Holy Ghost. I. Pet. 1:2, 11, 12, 23.

The three Persons of the Trinity. I. Pet. 1 : 2.

The Father and Christ. I. Pet. 1 : 3.

The triune God. I. Pet. 1: 5, 21.

Twelfth: Examine carefully the remaining chapters, and write out distinctly what Peter teaches with reference to the doctrine of God.

Thirteenth: Study carefully the second chapter, and note what Peter says of Christ as our Savior.

(1) He is gracious. I. Pet. 2: 3.

(2) The living stone, I. Pet. 2: 4; the chief corner stone, I. Pet. 2: 6, 7.

(3) Rejected of men. I. Pet. 2: 4, 7.

(4) Elect with God. I. Pet. 2: 4, 6.

(5) Precious. I. Pet. 2: 4, 6.

(6) Believers are acceptable to God through Jesus Christ. I. Pet. 2:5;

(7) He that believeth on Him shall not be ashamed. I. Pet. 2: 6.

(8) To unbelievers he is a stone of stumbling. I. Pet. 2: 8.

(9) For his sake we are to be subject to all human ordinances. I. Pet. 2:13.

(10) Christ has suffered for us. I. Pet. 2: 21.

(11) Has left us an example of sufferings. I. Pet. 2: 21.

(12) We are to follow in his footsteps. I. Pet. 2: 22.

(13) He sinned not in act. I. Pet. 2: 22.

(14) Nor in word. I. Pet. 2: 23.

(15) He committed Himself and His cause to God the Father. I. Pet. 2:23.

(16) He bore our sins in His own body. I. Pet. 2: 24.

(17) By His stripes we are healed. I. Pet. 2: 24.

(18) He is the Shepherd and Bishop of our souls. I. Pet. 2: 25.

(19) Peter believes in the vicarious atonement of Christ.

Fourteenth: Study the other chapters in the same way; write out the thought distinctly, compare, and draw up results in tabular form.

Fifteenth: Study the Epistle as a whole, section by section, with reference to its practical truths.

(1) Our duties to God.

(2) Our duties in the State.

(3) Our duties in the Family.

      (a) Servants.

      (b) Husbands.

      (c) Wives.

(4) Our duties as members of the Church.

(5) Our duties to self.

(6) The duties of a Pastor.

Sixteenth: Lillie's Lectures on I. and II. Peter especially recommended.

PART II.
The Four-fold Office of the Holy Ghost.

First: We may speak of a four-fold office of the Holy Ghost—
    (1) As convicting. John 16:8.
    (2) As teaching and witnessing. John 16:13-15.
    (3) As correcting. II. Tim. 3:16; Rom. 8:14.
    (4) As comforting. John 14:16; Rom. 8:26.

Second: The office of the Holy Spirit is to convict.
    (1) To bring out clearly the real state of things. John 3:20; Eph. 5:13.
    (2) By applying it to the particular person in question. James 2:9; Jude 15; II. Tim. 4:2.
        (a) In chastisement. I. Tim. 5:20; Tit. 1:9.
        (b) Or with a view of restoration. Tit. 1:13; Heb. 12:5.

Third: This conviction is by means of the Word of God. II. Tim. 4:2; Tit. 1:13.

Fourth: The result of this conviction may be two-fold. II. Cor. 2:16.
    (1) Leading to conversion. I. Cor. 14:24, 25.
    (2) Leading to hardening and condemnation. Acts 24:25.

Fifth: The Spirit will convict the world (sinful men) of three things:
    (1) Of sin, because they believe not on Christ. John 16: 9.
        (a) As born in sin and by nature children of wrath. Eph. 2: 3.
        (b) As sinful, and therefore subject to death. Rom. 5:12.
        (c) As born of the flesh, and therefore requiring the new birth. John 3:5, 6.
        (d) As not possessing life, but in a state of spiritual death, with the wrath of God abiding on him. I. John 3:14; John 5:24; 3:36; Col. 1:13.

(e) That eternal life can only be had in believing in Christ. John 3: 6; 8:24; Acts 4:12; I. John 5:12, 13.

(f) That a willful rejection of Christ is not the only sin that condemns, but that as long as men are not in saving contact with Christ, they are under condemnation, guilty, and under the wrath of God. Rom. 1:18; 3:23 ; John 3:18, 36; 5:24; Rom. 5:1, 2.

(2) Of righteousness, because the life, death and resurrection of Jesus Christ has manifested a righteousness of God, which is to be obtained alone through faith in Jesus Christ. John 15:10; Rom. 3:21,22; Phil. 3:9.

(3) Of judgment, for judgment shall overtake all who do not obtain eternal life in Christ. John 3:18; 3:36; 5.24,29.

Sixth: The office of the Holy Spirit is to teach and to bear witness. John 14:26; 15:26.

(1) In the early Church there were special gifts of the Spirit. I. Cor. 12:4-11; John 16:13-15.

(2) All these passages give evidence of the inspiration of the Apostles and prophets of the New Testament.

(3) The Spirit now teaches us by means of the Word. II. Tim. 3:16, 17; Heb. 4: 12, 13.

(4) The Word, by means of the Spirit, begets faith in the hearer. I. Thess. 1:5: Rom. 10:17; I. John 2:20, 27.

(5) The Holy Spirit, through the Word, bears witness to the individual believer, that he is a child of God. Rom. 8:16; I. Cor. 2:11; I. John 5:10. 11.

Seventh: The Holy Spirit continues his work in the believer, by means of the word, in correcting and disciplining the heart. II. Tim. 3:16; I. Pet. 2:2.

(1) The Spirit leads us to mortify the deeds of the body. Rom. 8:14.

(2) We are to walk by the Spirit. Gal 5:16, 25.

(3) We are to be led by the Spirit Gal. 5:18.

(4) We are to walk after the Spirit. Rom. 8:4-14.

(5) The Spirit strengthens us in faith and love. Eph. 5:16-19.

Eighth: The Holy Spirit comforts.

(1) He fills the saints with joy. Acts 13:52; Rom. 14:17.

(2) Even while in affliction. I. Thess. 1:6.

(3) He imparts the love of God. Rom. 5:3-5.

(4) He imparts hope. Rom. 15:13; Gal. 5:5.

(5) The Spirit, by means of the regenerated human spirit, carries on his operations in the words, acts, prayers, and sighs of the saints. Rom. 8:26.

STUDY XV.
The Second Epistle of Peter.

First: We will first speak of the canonicity of this Epistle.

(1) By the canonicity of a book, we mean that it has a right to belong to the New Testament, as a rule of our faith and conduct.

(2) The collection of the New Testament Canon was relatively late in its origin, and slow in its progress.

(3) It was not until the third council of Carthage (397 A.D.) that the question of the Canon was finally closed.

(4) The Second Epistle of Peter does not seem to have been widely known in the Early Church, nor is it much quoted.

(5) In the time of Origen, died 254, it was, however, freely used, but not yet unanimously accepted into the Canon.

(6) It first appears as one of the Canonical Books in the canons of the Council of Laodicea, 366 A.D.

(7) We do not know why this Epistle was not more widely known during the second century, nor why there were doubts of its genuineness in the third and fourth centuries.

(8) We may rest assured that the Council of Laodicea had satisfactory proof, before they admitted this book into the Canon, that the Epistle was genuine, written by the person who professes to have written it.

Second: For the genuineness and authenticity of this Epistle, we have strong internal evidence.

Third: Read the Epistle carefully, and note what the writer states concerning himself.

(1) The writer's name is Simon Peter, 1: 1.

(2) An Apostle of Jesus Christ, 1: 1.

(3) Possesses precious faith and precious promises, 1:1,4.

(4) Has been called of God, and enjoys all things that pertain

to life and godliness, 1 : 3.

(5) Is anxious to write, and remind his readers of the duties of their calling, 1:12, 13, 15.

(6) Expects soon to die, 1: 13, 14, 15.

(7) The writer's death has been foretold by Christ, 1: 14; cf. John 21: 18, 19.

(8) Had before this made known to his readers the power and coming of Christ, 1: 16.

(9) Had seen Christ in person, 1: 16.

(10) Was present at the Transfiguration, 1: 18.

(11) Is certain of the truth of the Christian religion, 1: 19.

(12) Has written a former letter, 8: 1.

(13) Has the same object in view in both letters, 3: 1, 2.

(14) Knows of letters written by Paul to these same persons, 3:16.

Fourth: Read carefully a second time, and note what the writer says about the persons addressed.

(1) They are believers, 1: 1, 3, 4; brethren, 1: 10; beloved, 3: 8, 14, 17.

(2) Enjoy all spiritual blessings, 1: 3, 4, 8, 12; 3: 17.

(3) Have a knowledge of the truth, and are steadfast, 1: 12; 3: 17.

(4) Had heard Peter preach, 1: 16; 3:2.

(5) Are living among the Gentiles, 2: 18.

(6) Had received a former letter from the writer, 3: 1.

(7) As well as letters from Paul, 3: 15.

(8) Are acquainted with the Old Testament, 1: 20, 21; 2: 5-8.

(9) Among them false teachers shall arise, 2: 1-3.

(10) Many shall be led away, 2: 2.

Fifth: If we compare these results with those obtained from the study of I. Peter (see Study XIV), we have a right to infer that both were written by the same author.

Sixth: If we further compare the contents of both Epistles, we find they breathe the same spirit, and convey the same teaching.

(1) The writer of both thought that the end of the world was near, I. Pet. 1:5; 4:7; II. Pet. 3:3, 10-12

(2) The same stress is laid on prophecy, I. Pet. 1: 10-12, II. Pet.

1 : 19, 20.

(3) In both, reference to the history of Noah, I. Pet. 3: 20; II. Pet. 2:5; 3:6.

(4) On the nature and right use of Christian liberty, I. Pet. 2: 16; II. Pet. 2: 19.

(5) In both, Paul's teaching is recognized, I. Pet. 5: 12; II. Pet 3:15.

Seventh: The evidence that the same author wrote both Epistles becomes still stronger if we compare the actual words used in both Epistles.

Eighth: Make a special study of both Epistles, with this comparison in view, ("Precious," "grace and peace be multiplied," "add," "love of the brethren," "calling and election," "eye-witnesses," "without blemish or spot," etc.)

Ninth: The Epistle was evidently written by Peter sometime after his first Epistle, not long before his death, 63-67 A.D.

Tenth: Read the Epistle carefully, and divide into sections with appropriate headings.

(1) 1:1, 2. Address and greeting.

(2) 1: 3-11. Exhortation to grow in the graces of the spiritual life.

(3) 1:12-21. These exhortations confirmed by Apostolic testimony and Old Testament prophecy.

(4) 2: 1-22. Description of false teachers.

(5) 3: 1-7. The certainty of Christ's coming established.

(6) 3: 8-13. The end of the world.

(7) 3: 14-18. Exhortations with reference to the coming of the day of God.

Eleventh: Study carefully each section, and write out the thought as clearly and concisely as possible.

Twelfth: Study each section in detail, and write out distinctly what Peter teaches concerning the Father, the Son and the Holy Ghost.

(1) The Father is referred to, 1: 1, 2, 3, 17, etc.

(2) The Son is referred to, 1: 1, 2, 3. 8, 11, 14, etc.

(3) The Father and Son are named together and distinguished from each other, 1: 1, 2, 3.

(4) God is the source of all spiritual blessings, 1:3, 4.

(5) Jesus is Lord, 1: 8, 11, 14; 2: 20; 3: 2, 18.

(6) Jesus is the Savior, 1: 11; 2: 20; 3: 3, 18.

(7) Jesus has an eternal kingdom, 1: 11.

(8) Jesus has eternal glory, 3: 18.

(9) His power and majesty, 1: 16.

(10) Has received honor and glory from the Father, 1: 17.

(11) Is the beloved of the Father, 1: 17.

(12) Is called Master, 2: 1.

(13) The Holy Ghost is God, 1: 21.

(14) God created the heavens and earth by his Word, 3: 5.

(15) With God there is no time, 3: 8.

(16) He is faithful to keep his promise, 3: 9.

(17) Long suffering, 3: 9, 15; wishing that all should come to repentance, 3: 9.

Thirteenth: Analyze thoroughly II. Peter 1: 1-11, and summarize what Peter teaches concerning the Way of Salvation.

(1) By faith we obtain the righteousness of God, 1:1;

(2) And appropriate the precious promises, 1: 4;

(3) And become partakers of the divine nature, 1:4;

(4) Receiving grace and peace, 1 : 2;

(5) And indeed all things pertaining to spiritual life and godliness, 1:3.

(6) Faith is increased by a true knowledge of God and of Jesus our Lord, 1:2, 3, 6, 8;

(7) Faith has its fruits, 1: 5-9.

(8) By faith the believer has escaped from the corruption in the world, 1: 4;

(9) And cleansed from his old sins, 1: 9.

(10) God has called us by his own glory and might, 1: 3;

(11) But we must make our calling and election sure, 1: 10;

(12) The aim of the believers is the eternal kingdom of our Lord, 1:11.

Fourteenth: Study II. Pet. 2: 1-22, and note the errors of doctrine and of life against which Peter warns.

Fifteenth: Study carefully the histories of Noah, Lot, and Balaam.

Sixteenth: What practical lessons can be deduced from this chapter?

Seventeenth: Study the whole Epistle carefully, with reference to what Peter teaches about the Future Life.

    (1) The state after death before the judgment.

        1. There is a state or place where the evil angels are reserved for judgment, 2:4;

        2. There is a state or place where the unrighteous are kept under punishment unto the day of judgment, 2: 9;

        3. Among these are specially mentioned the ungodly of Noah's time, 2:5; and

        4. The inhabitants of Sodom and Gomorrah, 2:6,

        5. Even all who walk after the flesh, 2:10.

    (2) The Second Coming of Christ.

        1. He shall come with power and majesty, 1: 16;

STUDY XVI.
The First Epistle of John.

First: It was the universal belief of the Early Church that the Apostle John wrote this Epistle.

Second: With this agrees the internal evidence obtained by a close comparison of the Epistle with the Gospel of John.

> (1) There is the same emphatic repetition of fundamental words and phrases, as "abide," "be of God," "be of the truth," "be of the world," "truth," "love," "light," "darkness," "do sin," "do the truth," "eternal life," etc.
>
> (2) There are larger coincidences of expression. Compare I. John 1: 1 with John 1: 1, 14; 20: 27.
>
> I. John 1:2 with John 3: 11; 19: 35; 1: 1.
>
> I. John 1:3 with John 17: 21.
>
> I. John 1:4 with John 16: 24; etc., etc.

Third: It is highly probable that John wrote this letter in his old age, while at Ephesus.

Fourth: For it was the uniform belief of the Early Church that John ended his days in Ephesus, ruling the churches of Asia.

Fifth: For an outline of the life of St. John, see notes in Study

Sixth: Of his later life, we know nothing trustworthy.

> (1) The tradition of his preservation from the boiling oil and poison under the Neronian persecution.
>
> (2) His exile in Patmos.
>
> (3) His later residence at Ephesus.
>
> (4) The stories of the robber chief, of meeting Cerinthus, of the tame partridge, of his repeated exhortation, "Little children, love one another."

Seventh: This Epistle is a circular letter addressed to the Asiatic Churches, of which Ephesus was the center.

Eighth: It is addressed to those who had been carefully trained and had lived long in the faith.

Ninth: This Epistle is a companion to John's Gospel, the condensed moral and practical application of the Gospel.

Tenth: They both have the same object. Compare I. John 1:3; 5:13, with John 20: 31.

Eleventh: They both have the same special characteristics, sublimity of thought combined with simplicity of language.

Twelfth: The writer speaks throughout with the authority of an Apostle, I. John 1:1; 4: 14.

Thirteenth: Read the Epistle carefully, and divide into sections with appropriate headings.
  (1) Introduction, 1: 1-4.
  (2) The nature of fellowship with God. 1 : 5—2: 29.
      (a) What Walking in the Light involves. 1 : 5—2: 11.
          1. Fellowship with God and with the brethren (1:5-7).
          2. Consciousness and confession of sin (1: 810).
          3. The remedy for sin, and the sign that it is effectual
          (2:1-6).
          4. Love of the brethren (2: 7-11).
      (b) What Walking in the Light excludes. 2: 12-29.
          1. Three-fold statement of reasons for writing (2: 12-14).
          2. The things to be avoided,— the world and its ways (2: 15-17).
          3. The persons to be avoided,— Antichrists (2: 18-26).
          4. Christ the place of safety (2: 27-29).
  (3) The fruit of fellowship is holiness. 3: 1-24.

1. The children of God and the children of the Devil (3: 1-12).
2. Brotherhood in Christ and the hatred of the world (3: 13-24).

(4) The law of Fellowship is Truth. 4: 1-6.

(5) The life of Fellowship is Love. 4: 7-21.

(6) The root of Fellowship is Faith. 5: 1-21.

1. The power of the Christian life: the Victory and Witness of Faith (5: 1-12).
2. The activity and confidence of the Christian life: Epilogue (5: 13-21).

Fourteenth: Examine Epistle to see if above analysis is satisfactory, and correct if deemed necessary.

Fifteenth: Analyze I. John 1: 1-4, and compare with John 1:1-18.

(1) The subject-matter of the Gospel (1:13).

(2) The purpose of the Epistle (1:4).

Sixteenth: The two passages are not parallel, but complementary.

Seventeenth: St. John uses the plural, as speaking in the name of the Apostles, of which he was the last surviving representative.

Eighteenth: Analyze each section as already given, and write out each distinct thought.

Nineteenth: In I. John 1:5-10, note the contrast between Light and Darkness.

(1) Where there is light, there we find truth, righteousness, joy, safety, life.

(2) Where there is darkness, there we find falsehood, unrighteousness, sorrow, peril, death.

Twentieth: In I. John 1:6-10, we have a statement of the three false views which man may take with reference to sin.

(1) He may deny the true character of sin (1: 6, 7).

(2) He may deny that he has sin in him as an evil principle (1:8,9).

(3) He may deny that he personally has sinned (1: 10).

Twenty-first: Christ is not simply our Propitiator (4: 14), but also our Propitiation (2: 2), the propitiatory offering as well as the Priest (Horn. 3: 25; Eph. 5: 2), our life (Col. 3: 4), our righteousness, sanctification, and redemption (I. Cor. 1: 31).

Twenty-second: Compare the three evil tendencies in the world (I. John 2: 16) with the three elements in the temptation of Eve (Gen. 3. 6), and with the three temptations of our Lord (Luke 4: 12).

Twenty-third: In I. John 3: 13, 14, we have one of the five titles by which the followers of Christ are known in the New Testament. (See Westcott.)
(1) "The disciples," John 2: 11, 12; 6: 61, 66; Acts 6: 1, 2, 7; etc.
(2) "The brethren," Acts 1: 15; 9: 30; St. Paul throughout his Epistles; I. John 3: 14; III. John 5: 10; John 21: 23.
(3) "The believers," Acts 10: 45; I. Tim. 4: 12; etc.
(4) "The saints," Acts 9: 13, 32, 41; Jude 3; St. Paul throughout his Epistles.
(5) "Christians," Acts 11: 26; 26: 28; I. Pet. 4 16.

Twenty-fourth: A close analysis of I. John 4:7-21, shows us that this section deals in succession with:
(1) The ground of love (4: 7-10).
(2) The inspiration of love (4: 11-16 a).
(3) The activity of love (4: 166-21).

Twenty-fifth: St. John in his writings gives us three statements as to the nature of the Divine Being:
(1) God is spirit, John 4: 24.
(2) God is light, I. John 1:5.
(3) God is love, I. John 4: 8, 16.

Twenty-sixth: We are not to regard spirit, light, and love simply as attributes of God, but they describe essential aspects of his nature.
(1) God in his being is Spirit.
(2) By Light, we have a moral description of the character of God, in his relation to all created things.

(3) Love describes God in his personal relation to self-conscious creatures.

(4) We may therefore define God as Holy Love.

Twenty-seventh: Study the first chapter, and note what John teaches concerning the doctrine of God.

> (1) Of the Father.
>> 1. The origin of grace is in God the Father, 1: 2.
>> 2. The believer has fellowship with the Father, 1: 3.
>> 3. God as to his essential nature is perfect light, 1: 5.
>> 4. Therefore God is absolutely holy, 1:5.
>> 5. God is faithful, 1:9.
>> 6. God is righteous and true, 1: 9, 10.
>> 7. God the Father forgives and cleanses us by applying the blood of the Son to believers, 1: 9.
>
> (2) Of the Son.
>> 1. Jesus is the Christ, 1: 3.
>> 2. The Son of the Father, 1:3, 7.
>> 3. Of the same essence with the Father, 1: 3.
>> 4. Is the life, 1: 2.
>> 5. The believer has fellowship with him, 1: 3.
>> 6. Through the Son, the believer has fellowship with the Father, 1:3; 2:23.
>> 7. His blood cleanses us from all sin, 1: 7.
>> 8. This implies that he has died for us, 1: 7.

Twenty-eighth: In the same way study the whole Epistle, writing out clearly and arranging in tabular form, what John teaches concerning the three Persons of the Trinity.

Twenty-ninth: Study the first chapter, and note what John teaches concerning sin, and man's relation to God.

> (1) Eternal life has been manifested in Christ, 1: 2.
> (2) Outside of Christ there is no fellowship with God, 1:3. Compare I. John 3: 14; John 5: 24, 40; 3: 36; Eph. 2: 3.

STUDY XVII.
PART I.
The Second Epistle of John.

First: The testimony of the Early Church is strongly in favor of the view that the Gospel and the three Epistles were written by the Apostle John.

Second: This implies that the Apostle calls himself "the Elder," (II. John 1; III. John 1) not simply to describe his age or fatherly affection, but also his official position, as the last of the Apostles.

Third: Internal evidence is also strongly in favor of the Apostolic authorship of the Second, and therefore also of the Third Epistle.

(1) Compare II. John 1 and III. John 1 with I. John 3: 18.
(2) II. John 4 and III. John 3 with I. John 4: 21.
(3) II. John 5 with I. John 2: 7 and John 13: 34.
(4) II. John 7 with I. John 4: 1-3.
(5) II. John 9 with I. John 2: 23.
(6) III. John 11 with I. John 2: 29; 3: 6.
(7) III. John 12 with John 21: 24.
(8) III. John 13, 14 and II. John 12, 13, with I. John 1: 4 and John 15: 11.

Fourth: This Epistle shows the Apostle John to us as the shepherd of individual souls.

Fifth: In it we have a glimpse of the everyday life of the Christian home.

Sixth: Some think by the term "elect lady" some particular Christian Church is meant.

Seventh: But it is better to regard this letter as written to an individual, to some Christian lady, of whom we have no further information, save what this letter affords.

Eighth: The letter appears to have been written after his first Epistle, and probably from Ephesus.

Ninth: Read the letter carefully, and find out all you can about the person addressed.

Tenth: The Greek for "lady" is kuria, and some have thought that the name of the woman addressed by John was Eyria.

Eleventh: Make a careful analysis of the Epistle.
    (1) Address and greeting (1-3).
    (2) Counsel and warning (4-11).
        1. Occasion of the letter (4).
        2. Exhortation to love and obedience (5, 6).
        3. Warnings against false doctrine (7, 9).
        4. Warnings against false hospitality (10, 11).
    (3) Conclusion (12, 13).

Twelfth: There are forty-five variations in this Epistle between the Authorized and the Revised Versions. (Verify.) A reason can be given for each change in the translation.

Thirteenth: The word "truth" is used five times in this Epistle, and six times in III. John.

Fourteenth: The combination of the words "grace, mercy, and peace" occurs only in II. John 3; I. Tim. 1: 1; II. Tim. 1: 2.

Fifteenth: Make a special study of each of these three terms.
    (1) Grace designates the favor and conduct of God towards man as a sinner. See Study III., Part II.
    (2) The word "grace" is rare in the writings of John. Only here and John 1:14, 16, 17; Rev. 1:4; 22:21.
    (3) Mercy is the compassion of God towards man's misery as a sinner. It occurs only here in the writings of John.

(4) Peace is the result when the guilt of sin is forgiven. See John 14: 27; 16: 33; 20: 19, 21, 26; Rom. 8: 6; Eph. 2: 14.

Sixteenth: John lays great stress on the Incarnation of Jesus Christ. II. John 7.

Seventeenth: John in his writings describes the Incarnation under different aspects. (See Westcott).

(1) In regard to the Father, it is a "Sending."

(a) In general. John 5: 23, 37; 6: 44; 8: 18; 12: 49; 14: 24.

(b) With some special object expressed. John 3: 17; I. John 4: 9, 10, 14.

(2) In regard to the Son, it is a "Coming."

(a) The simple fact stated. John 1: 11; 8:42; 16: 28; I. John 4:2.

(b) With some special object designated. John 9: 39; 10: 10:12:47; 18:37.

(3) In regard to the form, it is in "Flesh."

(a) The simple fact stated. John 1 : 14; I. John 4: 2.

(b) He shall so come again, II. John 7.

(4) In regard to men, it is a "Manifestation."

(a) He was manifested by his Incarnation. John 1:31; I. John 1:2; 3:5, 8.

(b) He was manifested in his glorified body, after his resurrection. John 21: 1, 14.

(c) He shall be manifested in the future. I. John 2: 28; 3: 2.

Eighteenth: Scripture clearly teaches why the Son of God became Man.

(1) That he might save us from the condemnation of sin.

(a) To save sinners. I. Tim. 1: 15.

(b) To seek and to save that which was lost. Luke 19: 10.

(c) To redeem them which were under the law. Gal. 4: 4, 5; 3:13.

(2) That by a vicarious sacrifice he might satisfy the holiness and justice of God.

(a) To give his life a ransom for many. Matt. 20: 28; Heb. 9:28.

(b) To make propitiation for the sins of the people, Heb. 2:17; Rom. 3:25; I. John 2: 1, 2; 4: 10.

(c) To take away sins, I. John 3: 5; 1.9.

(d) To redeem us with his precious blood, I. Pet. 1 : 18-20.

(3) That he might conquer Satan.

(a) To destroy the works of the devil. I. John 3: 8.

(b) To bring to nought him that had the power of death, that is, the devil. Heb. 2: 14.

(4) That he might bestow upon us eternal life. John 3:16; 10:10.

PART II.
The Third Epistle of John.

First: This letter appears to have been written by John about the same time as the Second Epistle, after the Gospel and First Epistle, towards the end of the Apostle's life.

Second: Of Gaius, the person addressed, we know nothing definite, save what this letter informs us.

Third: It is highly probable that there are at least three persons of the name of Gaius, mentioned in the New Testament.
> (1) Gaius of Corinth (Rom. 16: 28), probably the same as the one mentioned in I. Cor. 1: 14.
> (2) Gaius of Macedonia. Acts 19: 29.
> (3) Gaius of Derbe. Acts 20:1

Fourth: It is possible that the Gaius of our Epistle may be one of these.

Fifth: Read the Epistle carefully, and note what we can learn concerning Gaius.
> (1) He is a believer (v. 2) and beloved of the Apostle (v. 1).
> (2) Setting a good example to other believers (vv. 3, 4).
> (3) Noted for his hospitality to Christian strangers (vv. 5-7).
> (4) The Apostle hopes shortly to visit him (v. 14).
> (5) Is well-known (v. 14).
> (6) Possibly some well-to-do layman (v. 6).
> (7) A prominent member of some local Church (v. 9).

Sixth: Make a careful analysis of the Epistle.
> (1) Address (1).
> (2) Personal good wishes (2-4).

(3) Gaius is commended for his hospitality to missionary brethren (5-8).

(4) Diotrephes is condemned for his ambitious self-assertion (9, 10).

(5) Demetrius is commended (11, 12).

(6) Conclusion (13, 14).

Seventh: Make a special study of the titles given to our Savior in the Epistles of John. (See Westcott.)

(1) "The Name." III. John 7; compare Acts 5: 41; John 20: 31; I. John 2: 12; 3. 23.

(2) "Jesus." I. John 2: 22; 4: 3; 5: 1, 5.

(3) "Christ." II. John 9.

(4) "Jesus Christ." I. John 2: 1; 5:6; II. John 7.

(5) "The Son." I. John 2: 22, 23, 24; 4: 14; 5: 12.

(6) "The Son of God." L John 3: 8; 5: 10, 12, 13, 20.

(7) "Jesus his Son." I. John 1: 7.

(8) "His only begotten Son." I. John 4: 9.

(9) His full title, "His Son Jesus Christ," is found three times, I. John 1:3; 3:23; 5:20.

Eighth: St. John, in his writings, uses the word "truth" in various senses. (See Alexander in Speaker's Commentary.)

(1) Truth as objective,

(a) As living and embodied in the Son. John 14: 6.

(b) As living and embodied in the Holy Spirit. I. John 5:7.

(c) As embodied in the sum-total of the revelation of Jesus the absolute truth. John 1: 17; 8: 32, 40; 1G: 13; 17: 17.

(2) The truth received passes subjectively into the truth in us. I. John 1 : 8; 2: 4; II. John 2; III. John 3

(a) Truth in thought. I. John 2: 21; II. John 1.

(b) Truth in action. I. John 1 : 6.

(c) Truth in speech. John 8: 45, 46.

(d) Truth in actuality—the fact as opposed to the sham. I. John 3: 18; II. John 1; III. John 1.

STUDY XVIII.
The Epistle of Jude.

First: The writer of this Epistle was Jude, a brother of James, and therefore one of the brethren of the Lord.

Second: He was not one of the Apostles (John 7: 5), and probably was not converted to a belief in Jesus as the Messiah until after Christ's appearance to James, after the Resurrection. I. Cor. 15:7.

Third: Of his life we know absolutely nothing.

Fourth: The Epistle is addressed to Christians who had been Jews.
(a) His readers are familiar with Old Testament Scriptures and Jewish traditions.

Fifth: There is no reason to question the authenticity and genuineness of the Epistle.
(a) It is mentioned in the Muratorian Canon. (About 170 A.D.)
(b) Clemens of Alexandria (died 202) quotes it.
(c) It was received among the Canonical Books at the Council of Laodicea (363 A.D.), as well as at the Council of Carthage (397 A.D.)

Sixth: It was probably written in Palestine, shortly after Peter wrote his Second Epistle.

Seventh: A careful comparison of the Epistle of Jude with the Second Epistle of Peter, seems to establish the fact that II. Peter was written first.
(1) That which Peter predicts has already come to pass when Jude writes.
(1) Compare II. Pet. 2: 1, 2, 3, with Jude 4.
(2) Compare II. Pet. 3: 1-4, with Jude 17, 18.

(2) The evil teaching of which Peter speaks has already in Jude found its natural consequence of evil doing. Compare II. Pet. 2: 1-3 with Jude 4, 8, 10, 13, 16.

(3) Jude elaborates some of the passages of Peter. Compare II. Pet. 2: 4 with Jude 6; II. Pet. 2: 6 with Jude 7; II. Pet. 2: 11 with Jude 9; II. Pet. 2: 17 with Jude 12.

Eighth: Make a careful analysis of the Epistle.

Ninth: Analyze each verse, and write out each distinct thought.

Tenth: Make a special study of the following phrases: "Servant of Jesus Christ," "to them that are called," "kept for Jesus Christ," "our common salvation," "to contend for the faith," "the grace of our God," "the judgment of the great day," "the punishment of eternal fire," "the creatures without reason," "works of ungodliness," "ungodly sinners," "in the last time," "having not the Spirit," "your most holy faith," "praying in the Holy Spirit," "keep yourselves in the the love of God," "the mercy of our Lord Jesus Christ," "who are in doubt," "snatching them out of the fire," "the garment spotted by the flesh," "without blemish."

Eleventh: Make a special study of the following words: "Mercy," "peace," "love," "saint," "condemnation," "Master," "Lord," "Jesus," "Christ," "darkness," "error," "convict," "ungodly," "Apostle," "eternal life," "joy," "Savior," "glory," "dominion."

Twelfth: Prepare a brief historical sketch of all the facts which will explain the allusions of Jude to events recorded in the Old Testament.
(1) The Lord saved a people out of the land of Egypt.
(2) He destroyed them that believed not.
(3) The history of Sodom and Gomorrah.
(4) The way of Cain.
(5) The error of Balaam.
(6) The gainsaying of Korah.
(7) The history of Enoch.

Thirteenth: Jude takes it for granted that his readers are acquainted with certain facts of revelation not recorded in the Old Testament.
(1) The fall of the angels. Jude 6.

(2) The contention of Michael the archangel with the devil concerning the body of Moses. Jude 9.

(3) The prophecy of Enoch. Jude 14, 15.

Fourteenth: This ought not to surprise us, for Paul also gives us some facts in the history of Moses, not recorded in the book of Exodus. II. Tim. 3: 8.

Fifteenth: The very fact that the Apostle Jude uses these illustrations proves that the events referred to are historical and authentic.

Sixteenth: Because Jude refers to these events, it does not follow that he quotes from two apocryphal books known as the "Assumption of Moses" and the "Book of Enoch." books which may have existed in the time of Christ.

Seventeenth: For these two apocryphal books evidently are based upon the same true Jewish tradition.

Eighteenth: Make a special study of what the New Testament teaches concerning "Evil Angels." Jude 6.

    (1) From Jude 6, compared with II. Pet. 2:4, we learn:

        1. That the evil angels have sinned. II. Pet. 2: 4.

        2. And not kept their own principality. Jude 6.

        3. But left their proper habitation. Jude 6.

        4. God spared them not, but cast them into dungeons. II. Pet. 2:4.

        5. Into Tartarus. II. Pet. 2: 4.

        6. Committing them to pits of darkness. II. Pet. 2: 4.

        7. "Where the Lord keeps them in everlasting bonds. Jude 6.

        8. Under darkness. Jude 6.

        9. To be reserved unto the judgment of the great day. II. Pet. 2:4; Jude 6.

    (2) From other passages of Scripture we learn:

        1. That they are the angels of the devil. Matt. 25: 41; Rev. 12:7.

        2. For which the eternal fire is prepared. Matt. 25: 41.

3. The evil spirits, the demons, which in Christ's time possessed the souls and bodies of men. Acts 16: 12, 13; Matt. 12: 27, 28; etc.

4. The principalities, the powers, the world rulers of this darkness, against whom we wrestle: Eph. 6: 12; Col. 2: 15.

5. The spiritual hosts of wickedness in the heavenly places. Eph. 6: 12.

6. They seek to separate us from the love of God. Rom. 8: 38, 39.

7. In some way believers shall take part in their judgment. I. Cor. 6:3.

8. They have become subject to Christ. I. Pet. 3: 22.

9. They believe that there is a God, and shudder. James 2:19.

10. And acknowledge the justice of their doom, James 2:19; II. Pet. 2:11.

Nineteenth: Make a special study of what the New Testament teaches concerning "the devil." Jude 9.

    (1) His chief names.

        (a) The Tempter. Matt. 4:3; I. Thess. 3: 5.

        (b) Satan = Adversary = Enemy. Mark 1:13; 4:15; Acts 26: 18; Matt. 13: 39; I. Pet. 5: 8.

        (c) The Devil = Slanderer = Accuser. Rev. 12: 9, 10.

        (d) Old Serpent = Dragon. Rev. 12: 9; 20: 2; II. Cor. 11:3.

        (e) Beelzebub. Matt. 12: 24, 27.

    (2) His personal existence. The personal existence of the "Evil Spirit" is most distinctly taught in Scripture.

        (a) He was a murderer from the beginning. John 8: 44.

        (b) A liar, and the father of lies. John 8: 44.

        (c) He sinneth from the beginning. I. John 3: 8.

        (d) The Son of God was manifested that He might destroy the works of the devil. I. John 3: 8.

        (e) He is the prince of this world. John 14: 30; 16: 11; II. Cor. 4:4.

    (3) His nature.

        (a) He is a spirit. Eph, 2: 2.

(b) The whole description of his power implies spiritual nature and spiritual influence. Col. 1: 13; Eph. 2: 2; 6: 11; II. Cor. 11:14.

(c) Angels are subject to him. Matt. 25- 41; Rev. 12: 7, 9.

(d) The description given of his character also proves that he is of angelic nature, a rational and spiritual creature. Pride, I. Tim. 3: 6; craftiness, II. Cor. 11: 3; I. Tim. 3: 7; deceitfulness, Eph. 6: 11; fierce and powerful, I. Pet. 5: 8; presumptuous, Matt. 4: 5, 6.

(4) His mode of action.

(a) He acts directly upon the soul. Matt. 13: 19, 25, 39.

(b) He acts indirectly by his instruments. Eph. 6: 12; John 16: 11; II. Cor. 4:4; I. John 2: 16; John 8: 44; I. John 3: 10.

(c) But he can be resisted. Eph. 4:27; 6:11; James 4:7; I. Pet. 5.8.

(5) His doom. .

(a) He has been overcome. Luke 10: 18; Heb. 2: 14; I. John 3:8.

(b) He shall be bound for a thousand years. Rev. 20: 2, 3.

(c) And finally shall be cast into the lake of fire and brimstone. Matt. 25: 41; Rev. 20: 10.

Twentieth: In the Epistle of Jude we have a remarkable description of the different aspects of sin.

(1) In its manifestation.

1. It turns the grace of God into lasciviousness (v. 4).
2. Causes a denial of our Master and Lord (v. 4).
3. Leads to sins of abomination (v. 7).
4. To a defilement of the flesh (v. 8).
5. To a setting at nought of dominion (v. 8).
6. A railing at supernatural powers (v. 8).
7. At whatsoever things they know not (v. 10).
8. Leads to the deepest excesses of sin (vv. 10, 19).
9. Leads to hatred and murder (v. 11).
10. To wrong-doing for the sake of hire (v. 11).
11. And rebellion against the ministers of God (v. 11).
12. Makes men to be ungodly (vv. 4, 15).

13. To do works of ungodliness (v. 15).

14. To speak against the Lord (v. 15).

15. It leads men to murmur and complain (v. 16).

16. To walk after their ungodly lusts (vv. 16, 18).

17. To speak great swelling words (v. 16).

18. To shew respect of persons for the sake of advantage (v. 16).

19. Leads to mockery of God (v. 18).

20. To the making of separations (v. 19).

21. They have not the Spirit (v. 19).

(2) As compared with natural objects, these ungodly men are like:

1. The creatures without reason (v. 10).

2. Hidden rocks and spots in your love-feasts (v. 12).

3. Shepherds that without fear feed themselves (v. 12).

4. Clouds without water, carried along by winds (v. 12).

5. Autumn trees without fruit, twice dead, plucked up by the roots (v. 12).

6. Wild waves of the sea, foaming out their own shame (v. 13).

7. Wandering stars (v. 13).

(3) In its results.

1. For sin leads to condemnation (v. 4).

2. Those that believe not shall be destroyed (v. 5).

3. Shall be kept under darkness unto the judgment of the great day (v. 6).

4. Doomed to suffer the punishment of eternal fire (v. 7).

5. For whom the blackness of darkness has been reserved forever (v. 13).

6. Judgment shall be executed upon them (v. 15).

7. They shall be convicted of all their ungodly works (v. 15).

8. They shall be separated from the love of God (v. 21).

9. And cannot look for the mercy of our Lord Jesus Christ (v. 21).

10. They shall not obtain eternal life (v. 21).

11. They shall not dwell in the presence of the glory of God (v. 24).

12. They shall not possess exceeding joy (v. 31).

STUDY XIX.
The Book of Revelation.

First: It is the unanimous opinion of all conservative critics that the Book of Revelation was written by the Apostle John. Rev. 1:1, 4,9; 22:8.

Second: Early tradition points to Ephesus as the scene of the later activity of John.

Third: The time of John's exile to Patmos is uncertain.

Fourth: The majority of modern critics maintain that John wrote this book between 68 and 70 A.D. , before the destruction of Jerusalem.

Fifth: But there is no reason why we should doubt the clear and weighty testimony of the Early Church, that John wrote the book of Revelation in his old age, at the end of Domitian's reign, at about the same time that he wrote the Gospel and the Epistles.

Sixth: Some have laid great stress upon the difference in form and style between the Apocalypse and the other writings of John.

Seventh: But the extent of this difference has been greatly exaggerated, and whatever difference there may be, can all be traced to the grandeur of prophetic language.

Eighth: For it is plainly evident that John has intentionally adopted the prophetic style of Ezekiel and Daniel.

Ninth: Carefully read the Book of Revelation at one sitting, and test the following analysis of Farrar:
>   Prologue. Rev. 1:1-8.
>   (1) Letters to the Seven Churches in Asia. Rev. 1: 9—3: 22.

(2) The Seven Seals. Rev. 4:1-8:1.

(3) The Seven Trumpets. Rev. 8: 2—11: 19.

(4) The Seven Mystic Figures. Rev. 12: 1—14: 20.

    1. The Sun-clothed Woman. Rev. 12: 1-12.

    2. The Red Dragon. Rev. 12: 7-12.

    3. The Man-child. Rev. 12: 13-17.

    4. The First Beast from the Sea. Rev. 13: 1-10.

    5. The Second Beast from the Land. Rev. 13: 11-18.

    6. The Lamb on Mount Zion. Rev. 14: 1-13.

    7. The Son of Man on the Cloud. Rev. 14: 14-20.

(5) The Seven Vials. Rev. 15: 1—16: 21.

(6) The Doom of the Foes of Christ. Rev. 17: 1—20: 15.

(7) The Blessed Consummation. Rev. 21 : 1—22: 7.

(8) The Epilogue. Rev. 22 : 8-21.

Tenth: It is not our object to expound the Book of Revelation.

Eleventh: Amidst all the various theories of interpretation, it is well to remember that every prophecy is an enigma before its accomplishment.

Twelfth: There are three principal systems of exposition, according to which the Apocalypse has been interpreted.

    (1) The Preterists assert that these prophecies were fulfilled in the first ages of Christianity, chiefly in the history of the Jewish nation, down to the destruction of Jerusalem, and in the history of Pagan Rome.

    (2) The Continuous-Historical School maintains that the book contains a prophetic history of the continuous fortunes of the Church and of the World, from the time the book was written unto the end of all things — that many of the prophecies have been fulfilled, but that others are still unfulfilled.

    (3) The Futurists are divided into two classes:

        (a) The extreme Futurists, who maintain that the whole of the book, including the description of the Seven Churches, refers to what is still future.

        (b) The simple Futurists think that the first three chapters relate to actual churches existing in Asia Minor at the time of the writer, while the remaining prophecies are still unfulfilled.

Thirteenth: The book seems to decide for us how we are to view its contents. Rev. 1: 1, 19; 4: 1.

Fourteenth: In general, we may say that from Rev. 4: 1 onward, we have a description of what was future, not only in John's time, but also of that which now still largely lies in the future.

Fifteenth: Another important question is whether we are to regard the main body of the book (Rev. 4: 1—22: 7) as strictly continuous, following one after another in chronological order, or whether some of the visions are synchronous, each group containing a prophecy reaching from the prophet's time to the end of the world.

Sixteenth: There are many who think that the prophet at least five times, gives us a description of the end. (1) Rev. 6: 12-17; (2) Rev. 11:15-19; (3) Rev. 14:18-20; (4) Rev. 16:17-21; (5) Rev. 20: 11-15.

Seventeenth: This would favor the view that there at least five groups of visions, which, in a general way, refer to events parallel to one another, each one culminating in a vivid description of the final end.
    (1) Rev. 5: 1—8:1.
    (2) Rev. 8: 2—11:19.
    (3) Rev. 12: 1—14: 20.
    (4) Rev. 15: 1—16: 21.
    (5) Rev. 17: 1—20: 15.

Eighteenth. Make a careful analysis of the first chapter.

Nineteenth: Make a careful analysis of chapters two and three.

Twentieth: Note that the letters to the Seven Churches have a common seven-fold analysis:
    (1) The Address.
    (2) The description of the Speaker.
    (3) The praise.
    (4) The reproof.
    (5) The warning.
    (6) The solemn appeal.
    (7) The promise to him that overcometh.

Twenty-first: Examine carefully the first three chapters, verse by verse, and write out, as concisely as possible, what we learn about God the Father.

Twenty-second: Arrange in tabular form whatever is said of Jesus Christ, as presented in these three chapters.

Twenty-third: Study these three chapters with reference to what they teach about the Future.

Twenty- fourth: Study the same, verse by verse, with reference to the practical truths taught.
> (1) Duty to God.
> (2) Duty to man.
>> (a) In the State.
>> (b) In the Church.
>> (c) In the Family.
> (3) Duty to Self.

Twenty-fifth: Study the contents of each chapter so closely as to be able to give outline from memory.

STUDY XX.
PART I.
Practical Hints.

First: Constant review is the only key to exact knowledge.

Second: Progress does not depend on the amount of work gone over, but on retaining definitely the most important facts and truths learned.

Third: Above all other things it is necessary for the Christian worker to be familiar with the Bible.

Fourth: We cannot lay too much stress upon the necessity of committing the most important passages of God's word to memory.

Fifth: Make your own brief analysis of each book of the New Testament. Write it out as concisely as possible and commit to memory, and review constantly.

Sixth: Study one book at a time, analyze each chapter, and master so thoroughly that you can give the contents of each chapter from memory.

Seventh: Do not be discouraged at your slow progress. Remember it will be of greater help to you to know one book thoroughly, than to know many books but partly.

Eighth: Where there is a will there is a way. It is best to study by analysis and to work out your own results.

Ninth: If you begin to analyze, you will soon learn to arrange and put together in tabular form, which we call Synthesis.

Tenth: In these twenty studies we have aimed to give you hints how to study for yourselves.

Eleventh: Although these studies do not cover any of the Epistles of Paul, you will find that the hints given will be a sufficient guide.

Twelfth: It may sound somewhat strange to you, but if you simply follow the suggestions given in these twenty studies, you will have more than you can accomplish in a year.

Thirteenth: And what is the most important of all, you will not be studying the books of men, but the Word of God itself.

Fourteenth: Always remember that you are studying the Word for a double purpose:
    (1) For your own edification.
    (2) For the obtaining of power and wisdom to lead others to Christ.

Fifteenth: Let your aim be to apply whatever you learn in practical work.

Sixteenth: Commit especially those passages of God's Word which have a direct bearing on the salvation of souls.

Seventeenth: Be diligent in using the three means of Biblical study :
    (1) Prayer.
    (2) Meditation.
    (3) Christian experience.

Eighteenth: In the following Review do not take up a new subject until the preceding is absolutely mastered. Aim to be accurate. Go over this review at least once every year.

PART II.
REVIEW.
Questions Bearing on Introduction.

STUDY I.

1. Give the order of the books of the New Testament with number of chapters.

2. Name the Epistles of Paul in chronological order.

3. How do we prove that the books of the New Testament were written by the persons whose names they bear?

4. How do we know that our copies of the New Testament are correct and accurate?

5. Name the principal English versions of the New Testament.

6. Why do we find so many differences between the Authorized and Revised Versions?

STUDY II.

7. With what faculties should the student be endowed?

8. What dispositions should he cultivate?

9. What duties must he diligently perform?

10. Draw some distinctions between reading and studying the Bible.

11. Give some general hints for the study of the Gospels.

12. Give some general hints for the study of the Pauline Epistles.

13. Give some special suggestions for the study of one of the Epistles of Paul, say, the Epistle to the Colossians.

14. Under what heads may all our duties be classified?

15. Under what seven heads may all the truths of God's Word be classified?

16. What special doctrines belong to each great division?

STUDY III.

17. What five fundamental principles do we take for granted, when we interpret the Bible?

18. What is meant by the grammatical sense of Scripture?

19. What are our four sources for obtaining the true meaning of a passage?

20. Give some hints how to study a passage.

21. What help can we obtain from the context?

22. Why must we study parallel texts?

23. What advice would you give about using other resources?

24. What other circumstances must be taken into consideration in the interpretation of the Bible?

25. Why do we lay so much stress on the comparative study of the Bible?

26. How long does it take to read the different books of the New Testament?

STUDY IV.

27. Name five false views of the nature of the Inspiration of the Bible.

28. What do we mean by Plenary or Full Inspiration?

29. Distinguish between Revelation, Inspiration and Spiritual Illumination.

30. Why is it necessary that the Bible should be inspired?

31. Show from the Scriptures that the Bible is inspired.

STUDY V.

32. What are the two eyes of history?

33. Give a chronology of the life of Christ.

34. Give a chronology of the life of Paul.

35. Review thoroughly all the questions bearing on the geography of the places mentioned in the New Testament.

STUDY VI.

36. What is the practical value of a Harmony of the Gospels?

37. Review the seventy-eight questions given at the bottom of the Harmony.

STUDY VII.

38. Name the separate characteristics of the Four Gospels.

39. Write out a brief statement in answer to all questions pertaining to an "Introduction" to the Gospel according to Matthew, as "By whom written?" "For whom?" "When?" "Why?" "Where?"

40. Give the contents of each chapter from memory.

STUDY IX.

41. Why does the Gospel according to Mark, deserve to be studied first?

42. Write out a brief statement in answer to all questions pertaining to "Introduction."

43. Give the contents of each chapter from memory.

STUDY X.

44. Write out a brief statement in answer to all questions pertaining to an "Introduction" to the Gospel according to Luke.

45. Write out a brief history of Luke.

46. Give the contents of each chapter from memory.

STUDY XI

47. Show that the Apostle John was the author of the Fourth Gospel.

48. Write out a brief "Introduction" to this Gospel.

49. Name some of the peculiarities of this Gospel.

50. Give the contents of each chapter from memory.

51. Commit the following passages: John 3: 3-30; 5:19-47; 14:1-81; 15: 1-27; 16: 1-33; 17: 1-26.

52. Make a special and final study of the Harmony, asking yourself such questions as these:
    (1) What chapters in Mark and Luke correspond with the third of Matthew?
    (2) With the thirteenth?
    (3) With the twenty-first?
    (4) With the twenty-fourth?
    (5) In what Gospels is the Sermon on the Mount recorded?
    (6) What parables are common to the three Synoptists?
    (7) What are peculiar to Matthew, to Mark, to Luke?
    (8) What long passages are peculiar to Matthew, to Mark, to Luke, to John?

53. Examine yourself repeatedly on the contents of the different chapters.

54. Make a special study of Stalker's Life of Christ.

STUDY XII.

55. Write out a brief statement in answer to all questions pertaining to an "Introduction" to the Acts of the Apostles.

56. Give the contents of each chapter from memory.

57. Give an account of the principal speeches of Peter recorded in the Acts.

58. Give an account of the different missionary journeys of St. Paul.

59. Give an account of the principal speeches of Paul recorded in the Acts.

60. Give an account of the speech of Stephen.

61. Make a special study of Stalker's Life of St. Paul.

STUDY XIII.

62. Prepare a brief "Introduction" to the Epistle of James.

63. Write out a brief life of James, the Lord's brother.

64. Prepare your own analysis of the Epistle, commit to memory, and give the contents of each chapter from memory.

STUDY XIV.

65. Prepare a brief 'Introduction" to the Epistle of Peter.

66. Write out a brief life of Peter.

67. Prepare your own analysis of the Epistle, commit to memory, and give the contents of each chapter from memory.

STUDY XV.

68. What right have we to believe that II. Peter is a part of the New Testament?

69. What internal testimony have we for its genuineness and authenticity?

70. Prepare your own analysis, commit to memory, and give the contents of each chapter from memory.

STUDY XVI.

71. Write out a brief "Introduction" to the First Epistle of John.

72. Write a brief history of the life of John.

73. Prepare your own analysis of the Epistle, commit to memory, and give the contents of each chapter in your own words.

74. Commit to memory the following passages: 1. John 1:5-10; 2: 1-6; 2: 15-17; 3: 1-6; 4: 7-21.

STUDY XVII.

75. Write out a brief "Introduction" to the Second Epistle of John.

76. Write out a brief "Introduction" to the Third Epistle of John.

STUDY XVIII.

77. Write out a brief "Introduction" to the Epistle of Jude.

STUDY XIX.

78. Write out a brief "Introduction" to the book of Revelation.

79. Name the three principal theories of interpretation.

80. How may we analyze the book?

81. How may each of the letters to the Seven Churches be analyzed?

82. Give the contents of each chapter of the Book of Revelation.

Questions Bearing on the Doctrines and Duties of the Bible.

STUDY I.

1. In proving a doctrine from Scripture, it is not sufficient to state the general meaning of a passage, but quote Scripture correctly.

2. Commit at least two of the most important passages bearing on each doctrine.

3. Commit especially those passages having an immediate bearing on the salvation of souls.

4. Prove from Scripture that God has revealed himself as one God.

5. Prove that God has revealed himself as a Trinity in Unity.

6. Prove that the Holy Ghost proceeds from the Father and the Son.

7. What distinction between the persons of the Trinity may be drawn in outward works?

STUDY II.

8. Prove from Scripture that the Holy Ghost is a person.

9. Prove that the Holy Ghost is true God, of the same essence with the Father and the Son.

STUDY III.

10. What is meant by the grace of the Holy Spirit?

11. Why is the grace of God called the grace of the Holy Spirit?

12. What does the New Testament teach concerning the grace of the Holy Spirit?

13. Explain how the grace of God acts before conversion, in the act of conversion, and after conversion.

14. In what order may we speak of the works of grace?

STUDY IV.

15. What is meant by the call?

16. Distinguish between the direct and indirect call.

17. What does Christ teach us about the call?

18. What is the teaching of Peter?

19. What is the teaching of Paul?

STUDY V.

20. What is Paul's teaching of the condition of the natural man?

21. Define illumination.

22. Distinguish between illumination, regeneration, and sanctification.

23. What is the Scriptural teaching concerning illumination?

24. Distinguish between literal and spiritual illumination.

STUDY VI.

25. What is the teaching of Scripture concerning the new birth?

26. How is the new birth described?

27. In what twofold sense is the word regeneration used?

28. What distinction does St Paul draw between the condition of the intellect and will of man, before and after regeneration?

29. How is regeneration effected?

STUDY VII.

30. In what two-fold sense is conversion spoken of in Scripture?

31. Show that these Scripture passages are in harmony.

32. Describe the two parts of conversion.

33. How is conversion effected?

34. Make a special study of the Sermon on the Mount, and write out distinctly what Christ teaches.
      (1) About the kingdom of heaven.
      (2) About the members of the kingdom.
      (3) About entrance into the kingdom.
      (4) About himself and his work.
      (5) About the way of salvation.

35. The Miracles of Christ recorded in the Four Gospels, may be classified as follows:
      (1) Miracles on Nature.
            (a) Miracles of Creative Power.
            (b) Miracles of Providence.
      (2) Miracles on Man
            (a) Miracles of Personal Faith.
            (b) Miracles of Intercession,
            (c) Miracles of Love.
      (3) Miracles on the Spirit World.
            (a) Miracles of Intercession.
            (b) Miracles of Antagonism. (After Westcott).

36. Make a special study of the miracles recorded by Matthew, classifying them under the proper head.

37. Find out what miracles are recorded only by Mark, by Luke, by John.

STUDY VIII.

38. Distinguish between repentance and faith.

39. In what does repentance consist?

40. What are the marks of true repentance?

STUDY IX.

41. What are the three elements of faith?

42. Show that confidence is the principal part of faith.

43. Distinguish between general and special faith.

44. What is the contents of our faith?

45. Show that God is the efficient cause of our faith.

46. Show from Scripture what the instrumental cause of faith is.

47. Distinguish between the receptive and operative energy of faith.

STUDY X.

48. Prove from Scripture that justification is a judicial process.

49. Distinguish between justification, regeneration, and conversion.

50. Draw a contrast between the condition of man before and after justification.

51. In what two things does justification consist?

52. How has Christ obtained the forgiveness of our sins?

53. How has Christ obtained a righteousness for us?

54. In what does saving faith consist?

55. Distinguish between an imputed and an inherent righteousness.

56. Prove from Scripture that we are justified by faith alone.

57. What are the effects of justification?

58. Name certain properties of justification.

59. The Parables of Christ recorded in the Four Gospels may be classified as follows:

(1) Parables which represent the Kingdom of God as a Divine Power.
    1. The sower.
    2. The growing seed.
    3. The mustard seed.
    4. The leaven.
    5. The hid treasure.
    6. The pearl of great price.

(2) Parables which have respect to the Church as one whole.
    1. The barren fig tree.
    2. The wicked husbandmen.
    3. The great supper.
    4. The wedding garment.
    5. The wheat and the tares.
    6. The draw-net and the householder.

(3) Parables which refer to the entrance of individuals into the Church.
    1. The lost sheep.
    2. The lost piece of silver.
    3. The prodigal eon.

(4) Parables which relate to the faith of the members of the Kingdom.
    1. The laborers in the vineyard.
    2. The Pharisee and the publican.
    3. The friend at midnight.
    4. The unjust judge.
    5. The two sons.
    6. The rich man and Lazarus.
    7. The unprofitable servants.

(5) Parables which relate to the love of the members of the Kingdom.

    1. The unmerciful servant.

    2. The good Samaritan.

    3. The rich fool.

    4. The unjust steward.

    5. The two debtors.

(6) Parables which refer to the hope of Christians.

    1. The ten virgins.

    2. The talents.

    3. The pounds.

60. Make a special study of the first three classes of Parables.

61. Make a special study of the last three classes of Parables.

STUDY XL

62. Make a special study of John 1: 1-18, and write out what John teaches concerning the Person of Jesus Christ.

63. Make a special study of John 3:16-21, 31-36, and in a tabular form present what is taught with reference to the believer and unbeliever.

64. Study John 5:19-47, and present in tabular form what Jesus teaches concerning Himself.

65. Study John 10:1-18, and present in tabular form what Jesus teaches concerning Himself.

66. Study John 14:1-11, and present in tabular form what Jesus teaches concerning Himself.

67. Study John 14:15-31; 15:26—16: 15, and present in tabular form what Christ teaches concerning the Holy Spirit.

68. Study John 14:12-21; 15:1-27, and present in tabular form what Christ teaches concerning believers.

69. What is meant by the mystical union of the believer with Christ?

70. How is this union with Christ maintained?

71. When is the believer adopted as a son of God?

72. Present the Scriptural teaching of the believer's adoption as a son of God.

STUDY XII.

73. Arrange in tabular form and revise the theology of Peter, as taught in his speeches as recorded in Acts. (See statement Fourteenth).

74. Arrange in tabular form and revise the theology of Paul, as taught in his speeches as recorded in Acts. (See statement Seventeenth).

75. What is the New Testament teaching concerning a holy life?

76. How may we distinguish between renovation and sanctification?

77. Distinguish between Illumination, Regeneration, Conversion, Justification and Sanctification.

STUDY XIII.

78. Revise and rewrite your study of the Epistle of James with reference to its practical truths. (See statement Thirteenth.)

79. Present the New Testament teaching concerning Good Works.

80. Name the three Christian Virtues.

81. Name the four Cardinal Virtues.

82. Name the seven Spiritual Gifts.

83. The twelve fruits of the Spirit.

84. The seven Spiritual works of mercy.

85. The seven corporal works of mercy.

86. Name the seven deadly sins and their contrary virtues.

STUDY XIV.

87. Revise and rewrite what Peter teaches concerning the doctrine of God, as taught in his First Epistle. (See statements Eleven and Twelve).

88. Revise and rewrite what Peter teaches concerning the doctrine (1) of the Person and (2) of the work of Jesus Christ. (See statements Thirteen and Fourteen).

89. Revise and rewrite what Peter teaches with reference to the Practical Duties of the Christian. (See statement Fifteenth.)

90. What is the four-fold office of the Holy Ghost?

91. Present the Scriptural teaching of this four-fold office.

STUDY XV.

92. Study the Second Epistle of Peter carefully, with reference to what Peter teaches about the doctrine of man. (See Study II, p. 10.)

93. Study the whole Epistle with reference to the Practical Duties of the Christian, and present in tabular form.

STUDY XVI.

94. Study the First Epistle of John, and present what John teaches concerning the doctrine of God. (See Study II, p. 10.)

95. The doctrine of man. (See Study II, p. 10.)

96. The doctrine of the Person of Christ. (See Study II, p. 10.)

97. The doctrine of the work of Christ. (See Study II, p. 10.)

STUDY XVII.

98. Review carefully the whole study, and write out a summary of doctrinal teachings.

STUDY XVIII.

99. Summarize the doctrinal teachings of the Epistle of Jude.

STUDY" XIX.

100. Review and summarize the doctrinal teachings of the Book of Revelation.

STUDY XX.

101. Take up any one of the great central doctrines, as indicated in Study II., page 10, and make a special study, presenting it in the following form:
    (1) The teaching of Jesus, as given in the Gospels.
    (2) The teaching of Peter.
    (3) The teaching of James.
    (4) The teaching of Jude.
    (5) The teaching of John.

www.ingramcontent.com/pod-product-compliance
Lightning Source LLC
LaVergne TN
LVHW051555080426
835510LV00020B/2990